The Temple Cleansed

by
Colin D. Standish
President, Hartland Institute

and
Russell R. Standish
Founder, Remnant Ministries

Published by
Hartland Publications
P O Box 1, Rapidan, VA 22733, USA

ISBN 0-923309-29-2

The Temple Cleansed

1

1901 and 1903: Years of Destiny

F reshly back from her long term of service in Australia and New Zealand, Sister White attended the 1901 General Conference Session, her first for a decade. Many of the pioneer leaders of the church had passed away; others had reached their retirement years. The church was expanding rapidly, with membership now worldwide. The time had come for forward steps to be taken in the reorganization of the church. This need was a major issue in the mind of Sister White. On the opening day, she made this call:

> What we want now is a reorganization. We want to begin at the foundation, and to build upon a different principle (*General Conference Bulletin*, 1901, p. 25).

During this session, she soon came to the major point of issue.

> I want to say that from the light given to me by God, there should have been years ago organizations such as are now proposed. When we first met in conference, it was thought that the General Conference should extend over the whole world. But this is not in God's order (*General Conference Bulletin*, 1901, p. 68).

Noting the normal organizational pattern seen in worldly corporations, it was naturally thought that the General Conference should have authority over the whole of the work of God around the world. However, God is a decentralist; thus the whole issue of decentralization becomes pivotal to the counsel received by Sister White and transmitted to the delegates at the 1901 General Conference Session.

When Sister White explained the divine plan, it did not meet favor in the minds of many of the delegates. It was so alien to the accepted principles of organization that many leaders naturally saw it as tending towards disorganization and disunity. Nevertheless, Sister White assured the delegates that such would not be the case.

Conferences must be organized in different localities, and it
will be for the health of the different conferences to have it
thus. This does not mean that we are to cut ourselves apart
from one another, and be as separate atoms. Every conference
is to touch every other conference, and be in harmony with
every other conference. God wants us to talk for this, and He
wants us to act for this. We are the people of God, who are to
be separate from the world. We are to stand as representatives
of sacred truth (*General Conference Bulletin*, 1901, pp. 68,
69).

She explained further,

We want to understand that there are no gods in our conference. There are to be no kings here, and no kings in any
conference that is formed, "All ye are brethren." . . .

The Lord God of Israel will link us all together. The organizing of new conferences is not to separate us. It is to bind us
together. The conferences that are formed are to cling might-
ily to the Lord, so that through them He can reveal His power.
. . .

Remember that God can give wisdom to those who handle
His work. It is not necessary to send thousands of miles to
Battle Creek for advice, and then have to wait weeks before
an answer can be received. Those who are right on the ground
are to decide what shall be done. You know what you have to
wrestle with, but those who are thousands of miles away do
not know (*General Conference Bulletin*, 1901, p. 69, 70).

Sister White's counsel in 1901 was not new. The principles
had been laid down in earlier counsel.

As a people we should study God's plan for conducting His
work. Wherever He has given directions in regard to any
point, we should carefully consider how to regard His expressed will. This work should have special attention. It is not
wise to choose one man as president of the General Conference. The work of the General Conference has extended, and
some things have been made unnecessarily complicated. A
want of discernment has been shown. There should be a division of the field, or some other plan should be devised to
change the present order of things (*Testimonies to Ministers*,
p. 342).

There was an incipient attempt to follow this line of counsel before 1901.

> Hence, the European field came to be regarded as a self-sufficient continental unit, and it was called the "General Conference in Europe," while the organization in the land of origin was called the "General Conference in America." And there was beside, the Australasian Union Conference (*The Origin and History of Seventh-day Adventists*, Volume 3, p. 348).

Ellen White told the General Conference Session in 1901 that the limitations on control by the General Conference received the approbation of "the God of heaven and His angels" (*General Conference Bulletin*, 1901, p. 462).

This plan included no thought of the General Conference controlling operations around the whole world. The one purpose of such a decentralized approach to the administration of the church was to place Christ at the head of the church.

As Sister White warned on a number of occasions, the fewer people in control, the easier it is for Satan to take over the work. The more centralized the organization, the more opportunities there are for ungodly leadership to gain control. Once the work is centralized, it is much easier to politicize the work, and this will lead many men in leadership roles to feel that they are the direct representatives of God even when following the ways of Satan.

The 1901 plan for reorganization was built upon a spiritual base. Indeed, it was that organization which would allow the message of Christ our Righteousness to come into the lives of leaders and laity alike.

In 1897, responding to Sister White's counsels from Australia, the leaders separated the presidency of the General Conference Association and the presidency of the Mission Board from the presidency of the General Conference. In essence, that limited the role of the General Conference president in directing supervision of North America, for the Mission Board was responsible for the overseas work. Two different men were chosen for these roles.

The General Conference Bulletin for 1897 clarified the reasons for these changes.

We acknowledge the inconsistency . . . of centering so many responsibilities at Battle Creek and having so many matters of a varied character, and relating to work in widely different localities, submitted for consideration to a few men who largely compose our General Conference Committees and Boards. We also see that it is not wise to choose one man to preside over the varied interest and extensive territory of the General Conference (*General Conference Bulletin*, 1897, p. 89).

At the 1901 General Conference Session, it was desired that much greater reforms be made which would build upon that which took place in 1897. In North America, it was decided not to choose a General Conference president, but to choose a small committee which would choose itself a chairman every year. In 1901 the committee consisted of Dr. John Harvey Kellogg, Elder Alonzo T. Jones, and Elder Arthur G. Daniels. Elder Daniels was chosen as the chairman of the committee, but it was soon obvious that some in leadership disliked this new form of organization.

In a letter to Dr. Kellogg in 1902, Sister White wrote,

But the work that all heaven was waiting to do as soon as men prepared the way, was not done; for the leaders closed and bolted the door against the Spirit's entrance. There was a stopping short of entire surrender to God. And hearts that might have been purified from all error were strengthened in wrong doing . . . and said to the Spirit of God, "Go thy way for this time; when I have a more convenient season, I will call for thee" (Letter to J. H. Kellogg from Sister White, August 5, 1902).

Later, she wrote,

The result of the last General Conference has been the greatest, the most terrible sorrow of my life. No change was made. The spirit that should have been brought into the whole work as a result of that meeting was not brought in because men did not receive the testimonies of the Spirit of God. As they went to their several fields of labor, they did not walk in the light that the Lord had flashed upon their pathway, but carried into their work the wrong principles that had been prevailing in the work at Battle Creek (Letter to Judge Jesse Arthur From Sister White, Elmshaven, January 15, 1903; also found in *Manuscript Releases*, Volume 13, p. 122).

One of the most sobering statements that Sister White has ever made was made in relation to the 1901 General Conference Session. In *Testimonies for the Church*, Volume 8, pages 104-106, she reported a vision in which there was wonderful confession of sin, making right of all wrongs among the brethren, deep prayer, and calls for forgiveness; the Spirit of Christ was present, and a Pentecost-type atmosphere prevailed. However, as she regained consciousness, she wrote some of the most tragic words possible: "This might have been."

Unquestionably, had the leadership taken hold of the message of Christ Our Righteousness in 1888, they would have willingly and joyously accepted this decentralized organizational plan. However, with only a few accepting the 1888 message, there was a lack of willingness to go all the way with the reorganization, which was the second part of God's program for preparing His people for the end of time.

Of course, the principles outlined for the leadership of the work worldwide were not only meant for the upper echelons of the work, but also for all levels of our work through the conferences and through the church organization. While unions were formed in 1901, these were still significantly under the direction of the General Conference. Later, divisions of the General Conference were established, but they were just that, divisions of the General Conference. The leaders of each division, rather than having full authority to superintend, were seen to be vice-presidents of the General Conference, and therefore lacking the full authority that God wanted in His decentralized system of organization. The light that came to God's people at that time should have reflected upon the total direction of the Seventh-day Adventist Church ever since.

Of course, there is no reason why we today cannot follow the counsel that was given. However, the further away we get from 1901, the greater the likelihood of continuing in the old pathways rather than in the God-directed system of church governance.

At the 1903 General Conference, Elder A. G. Daniels set forth a proposal to place the mission board, the church's international organization, under the umbrella of the General Conference in America, with representations from around the world field. The

General Conference in Battle Creek would grow into the umbrella authority for the work around the whole planet, quite contrary God's counsel.

Percy T. Magan, then the dean of Emmanuel Missionary College, strongly opposed this plan. The minority report was rendered, in which Magan warned against opening the way for the papal form of church governance.

> But I want to say to you that any man who has ever read those histories, Leander's *History of the Christian Church*, Mosheim's or any other of the great church historians—any man who has ever read those histories can come to no other conclusion but that the principles which are to be brought in through this proposed constitution . . . are the same principles, and introduced in precisely the same way, as they were hundreds of years ago when the papacy was made. . . .

> I do not deny for a moment but what improvements have been made in the distribution of administrative power. I am heartily in favor of all that has been done in regard to union conferences, but I say that, as far as the head of things is concerned . . . the moment you vote, you have voted yourselves right back where we were two years ago and before it (Percy T. Magan, *General Conference Bulletin*, 1903, p. 150).

Magan was strongly supported by Elder E. A. Sutherland, president of Emmanuel Missionary College.

> I understood six years ago, when they elected their president of Europe, and also of Australia, and of this country, that those three men were supposed to be on the same plane* . . . and that, when a General Conference should be called, it would be the calling of all of these men from these three parts, and that no one of these presidents would be supposed to occupy any greater position than either of the others . . . I know that it was talked at that time that it should be so, and

---

* The 1897 action was confusing. For example, sometimes the European field was referred to as the "European General Conference," sometimes the "European Union Conference." An attempt in 1898 to clarify this action was just as confusing. At the 1901 General Conference, the term "European General Conference" was used; however, the articles of incorporation used the name "European Union Conference." Whatever name is correct, one fact is certain: God's plan was for the overseas areas to be free from the control of the General Conference in the United States.

this country was divided up into union conferences, or we called them districts at that time; but the plan was the same as we were following at the present time . . .

I believe, brethren, the thing to do is to go back where we were two years ago in the matter of reorganization, and take it up, and carry it out, and give it a fair trial, because those who have been in the responsible places have admitted that they did not carry out the letter of that, because they did not believe that it was possible. I believe that it is possible (E. A. Sutherland, *General Conference Bulletin*, 1903, pp. 168-169).

Sadly we note that the minority report was rejected, and the centralized plan gained great support. None other than a former General Conference President, Elder George Butler, exerted a strong influence toward centralization.

We are talking now on principles, brethren, and you will pardon one of the old hands, who has been in the work for so many years, and who has had the presidency of the General Conference for thirteen terms, for saying that he fails to see that anything of a kingly nature can be brought into it. I do not believe there can . . .

The difficulty in all of these things, I believe, is in regard to the principles being put in practice by the men that are placed in office . . . I cannot see a particle of danger in our old system of organization. . . .

If men will walk humbly before God, and remain willing to be instructed by the testimonies of His Spirit, they will never find anything wrong in the old system of organization brought out under the express influence of the Spirit of God . . . As one of the old hands, I see in this new constitution the same principles that we had in the beginning, that were endorsed by Sister White at the first. This is why I favor the new constitution (*General Conference Bulletin*, 1903, p. 163).

The irony of Elder Butler's statement was that, while he was referring to Sister White's statements, he was referring to what happened in 1863 when the work was confined more or less to the northeastern United States and a little of the Midwest. But now, as the work had expanded worldwide, Butler's comments opposed the counsel God had given. Butler could see nothing wrong with this plan. Nevertheless, it provided the advantage Satan desired in his attempt to derail the Seventh-day Adventist Church from its mission.

Had the brethren in 1901 and 1903 followed the divine counsel, they would have been following the counsel of the Lord. Christ gave wonderful counsel to the apostles. The mother of James and John coveted leadership responsibilities for her sons,

> Grant that these my two sons may sit, the one on thy right hand, and the other on the left, in thy kingdom (Matthew 20:21).

This request caused a bitter reaction from the other apostles.

> And when the ten heard it, they were moved with indignation against the two brethren (Matthew 20:24).

It was then that Jesus gave this divine counsel:

> But Jesus called them unto him, and said, Ye know that the princes of the Gentiles exercise dominion over them, and they that are great exercise authority upon them. But it shall not be so among you: but whosoever will be great among you, let him be your minister; And whosoever will be chief among you, let him be your servant: even as the Son of man came not to be ministered unto, but to minister, and to give his life a ransom for many (Matthew 20:25-28).

Christ stated that the concept of domination and authority is of pagan origin and is to be expected in the secular world. However, the principle of God's administration calls for the leaders to be the servants and ministers of the people. What a contrast!

James White put it correctly.

> And at no time during His public ministry does Christ intimate that any one of His disciples should be designated as their leader . . .

> There is no intimation that the apostles of Christ designated one of their number above another as their leader . . . The apostle exalts Christ as the great head of the church, and the only one to whom she should look for leadership, in Hebrews 12:1, 2.

Moses was simply a faithful servant in the Jewish house, while Christ is the Son over His own house. Moses was not a lord in the Jewish house. He was servant, while Christ was Lord . . .

Christ, then, is the leader of His people in all ages . . . But here we wish it distinctly understood that officers were not ordained in the Christian church, to order, or to command the church, and to "lord it over God's heritage" . . . Christ will lead His people, if they will be led (James White, *Review and Herald*, December 1, 1874).

In an editorial in 1881, just prior to his death, Elder White wrote,

It was not the design of God that any system of organization should exist in the Christian church that would take the leadership of Christ.

The minister who throws himself on any conference committee for direction, takes himself out of the hands of Christ. And when that committee takes into its own hands the work of directing the ambassadors for Christ, it takes the fearful responsibility. "One is your Master, even Christ, and all ye are brethren," Matthew 23:8. May God preserve to us our organization and form of church discipline in its original form (*Review and Herald*, January 4, 1881).

Eventually the delegates voted for the centralization of authority on April 11, 1903, with 85 delegates voting in favor, 20 delegates opposing, and 3 abstaining. There is little question that the delegates wanted a king to reign over them in much the same way that the Israelites of old desired a king. God, through His prophet, had warned Israel that this would lead to great trouble and burdens, but they still decided to go man's way rather than God's. God had warned that great difficulties would result and dangers occur if they placed such kingly authority in the hands of one man, but the people again chose the way of the world rather than the way of God.

Sister White responded to the new organization pointedly.

The heavenly Teacher inquired; 'What stronger delusion can beguile the mind than the pretense that you are building on the right foundation and that God accepts your works, when in reality you are working out many things according to worldly policy and are sinning against Jehovah? (*Testimonies for the Church*, Volume 8, p 249).

In 1903 the "upright" triangle of the hierarchical form of organization was given great impetus while the "inverted triangle" of representationalism was greatly weakened.

The time has come for the members of God's church to reexamine the true principles of church organization at the General Conference level and at all other levels of God's work. We have the right doctrines and message but these alone are not sufficient. We must also have the right way to implement them. Surely the apostasy within the church today is as much a result of abandoning the counsel of the Lord in organization as of rejecting the message of Christ our Righteousness.

2

The Peril of Kingly Power

It has ever been the object of Satan to induce men to look to other men rather than to God for their leadership. There seem to be, in every organization, those who want to exercise dominion and authority, and those who are anxious to submit unwaveringly to those who have authority and power. Knowing that these two groups complement one another, Satan continually seeks to effect an allegiance that will cause men entrusted with leadership responsibilities to believe that autocratic power is vested in them by God, and others to believe that such power is God-ordained. The latter, with great reverence and respect, believe that God requires them to be unwaveringly loyal to such individuals. Too often, they equate loyalty to God with loyalty to leaders. Quoted to support such a dangerous belief is the response of David when urged by his men to kill King Saul.

> And he said unto his men, The Lord forbid that I should do this thing unto my master, the Lord's anointed, to stretch forth mine hand against him, seeing he is the anointed of the Lord (1 Samuel 24:6).

The issue which led to David's response must be examined. He was refusing to do physical harm to the anointed of the Lord. This must not be interpreted to say that men should blindly follow leaders who, though anointed of the Lord, have turned their feet away from the pathway and direction of the Lord's counsel. We must rather follow the response of Peter and John when they were confronted with the choice between God-given responsibilities and the direction of human leaders.

> We ought to obey God rather than men (Acts 5:29).

We should not forget that blind loyalty to the Lord's anointed led men to cry, "Crucify Him!" These men believed that such loyalty to leaders constituted loyalty to God. What a deception! Yet are we different? Those who would show true loyalty to God and His anointed must place loyalty to their God as paramount.

While all respect and due courtesy pertain in our relationship with those who have leadership responsibility, it is dishonoring to God to blindly follow them or support them if they deviate from His express Word.

Perhaps the book *Testimonies to Ministers*, more than any other book, has been used to explain the relationship of leaders to the flock of God, and to warn against the dominating spirit which is apparent in the world.

Leaders are no less likely to reject God's counsel than are lay people. *Testimonies to Ministers* offers considerable counsel to leaders whose domineering influence has brought great anguish to the membership of the church.

> For years the church has been looking to man, and expecting much from man, but not looking to Jesus, in whom our hopes of eternal life are centered (*Testimonies to Ministers*, p. 93).

> Let me entreat our state conferences and our churches to cease putting their dependence upon men and making flesh their arm. Look not to other men to see how they conduct themselves under conviction of the truth . . . Our churches are weak because the members are educated to look to and depend upon human resources . . . (Ibid., p. 380).

> For years there has been a growing tendency for men placed in positions of responsibility to lord it over God's heritage, thus removing from church members their keen sense of the need of divine instruction and an appreciation of the privilege to counsel with God regarding their duty (Ibid., p. 477–478).

The Lord has also given other strong counsels relevant to this issue of kingly power.

> If the heart of the work becomes corrupt, the whole church, in its various branches and interests, scattered abroad over the face of the earth, suffers in consequence.

> Satan's chief work is at the headquarters of our faith. He spares no pains to corrupt men in responsible positions and to persuade them to be unfaithful to their several trusts (*Testimonies for the Church*, Volume 4, p. 210–211).

Jerusalem is a representation of what the church will be if it refuses to walk in the light that God has given. Jerusalem was favored of God as the depository of sacred trusts, but her people perverted the truth, and despised all entreaties and warnings. They would not respect His counsels (*Testimonies for the Church*, Volume 8, p. 67).

Unquestionably, James White and George Butler conflicted deeply concerning the correct role of the church. James White ever urged a decentralized approach where man looks to God rather than man for strength and for direction in spiritual matters. On the other hand, Butler believed that a centralized authority would bring spiritual strength, unity, and doctrinal purity to the church. Butler's conclusion is a strange one when we consider that the centrality of authority in the pope by the Roman Catholic Church has brought exactly the opposite result.

As early as 1873, ten years after the formation of the General Conference, Butler wrote,

There never was any great movement in this world without a leader; and in the nature of things it is impossible that there should be (*Review and Herald*, November 18, 1873).

On the other hand, James White wrote,

In the discussion of the subject of leadership, we propose to bring out evidence from the words of Christ, and from the teaching and practices of the early apostles, that Christ is the leader of His people, and that the work and office of leadership has not been laid upon any one person, at any one time, in the Christian age (*Review and Herald*, December 1, 1874).

The whole concept of decentralization is intimately linked with the issue of religious liberty. Much has been made of the eighteen talks given by E. J. Waggoner at the 1888 General Conference Session. These certainly were central to the message that was to be given, and is still to be given, to the world. However, much less is made of the fifteen talks given by A. T. Jones on religious liberty. These themes of Christ our Righteousness and religious liberty were inseparably linked, because freedom in Christ is inimical to religious oppression. Men and women must not place their eternal destiny in the hands of a man or a church, but

in the hands of God. Such a concept in no wise undermines the
divine role of the church in the life of God's people; it places the
church in its proper role under the authority of God.

Not long after the 1888 conference, A. T. Jones preached
thirty-one sermons in Kansas. Fifteen of these sermons were on
religious liberty, eleven were on church governance, and five were
on justification by faith. This gives some idea of Jones' linkage of
righteousness by faith, religious liberty, and church governance.

In his June 4, 1881 editorial, James White had written,

> The minister who throws himself on any conference commit-
> tee for direction, takes himself out of the hands of Christ
> (*Review and Herald*, January 4, 1881).

The conferences were not established to exercise dominion
over the ministry, nor over the local churches, but rather to plan
and expand the work of God in various regions and areas. Furthermore, the conferences were to act as counselors, not as dicta-
tors to the people of God. Sister White clearly expressed the
relationship between the 1888 message and church governance.

> Now, it has been Satan's determined purpose to eclipse the
> view of Jesus and lead men to look to man, and trust to man,
> and be educated to expect help from man. For years the church
> has been looking to man and expecting much from man, but
> not looking to Jesus, in whom our hopes of eternal life are
> centered. Therefore God gave to His servants a testimony that
> presented the truth as it is in Jesus, which is the third angels'
> message, in clear, distinct lines (*Testimonies to Ministers*, p.
> 93).

When men reject the full light of God's revealed will, they
inevitably try to exert power and domination in an attempt to get
allegiance in spite of apostasy. Sister White predicted the impotency of the church because of its failure to accept the 1888
message in all of its fullness.

> The peculiar work of the third angel has not been seen in its
> importance. God meant that His people should be far in ad-
> vance of the position which they occupy today . . . It is not in
> the order of God that light has been kept from our people—
> the very present truth which they needed for this time . . . If
> the leading men in our conferences do not now accept the

message sent them by God, and fall into line for action, the churches will suffer great loss (*Testimonies for the Church,* Volume 5, p. 714, 715).

Recognizing the terrible effect upon the laity as a result of this rejection of the message of 1888, Sister White wrote,

They began this satanic work at Minneapolis . . . Yet these men had been holding positions of trust, and have been molding the work after their own similitude, as far as they possibly could (*Testimonies to Ministers,* p. 79, 80).

The men in responsible positions have disappointed Jesus. They have refused precious blessings, and refused to be channels of light. . . . The knowledge they should receive of God . . . they refuse to accept, and thus become channels of darkness. The Spirit of God is grieved (*Manuscript 13,* 1889, p. 3, 4).

The tragedy is that these respected leaders had been placed in such a position that their wrong influence molded the ministry of younger men, so that a chain of apostasy commenced. The young men learned from the older men, and as the young men became more experienced, they, in turn, influenced the younger men following behind them.

Our young men look at the older men that stand still as a stick and will not move to accept any new light that is brought in; they will laugh and ridicule what these men say (Jones and Waggoner) and what they do as of no consequence. Who carries the burden of that laugh, and of that contempt, I ask you? Who carries it? It is the very ones that have interposed themselves between the light that God has given, that it shall not go to the people who should have it (*Sermons and Talks,* p. 124).

The Devil has been working for a year to obliterate these ideas (1888 message) . . . How long will the people at the heart of the work hold themselves against God? How long will men here sustain them in doing this work? Get out of the way, brethren. Take your hand off the ark of God, and let the Spirit of God come in and work in mighty power (Ibid., p. 126, 127).

Thus Satan used the leading men to pervert the minds of the younger ministers and, through them, the laity.

Already, a pattern of dependence upon humanity rather than upon the Word of God had shown itself within the Seventh-day Adventist Church. Leaders naturally tend to support and approve of those workers who look to them for leadership and counsel, seeing them as loyal and faithful. In reality, these workers may represent that group who have lost their confidence and loyalty to the Word of God and the truth of the gospel as a result of placing their loyalty in fallible, erring men. Once this situation commences, it is a most difficult process to reverse, for indeed the continuation of such a process leads to more and more error as one generation passes the torch of imperfect principles to the following generation. Once we have left the mountaintop of truth, the trend always progresses downhill, each generation taking the apostasy a little further than the generation before. This is exactly how Satan would have it. Every member of the Seventh-day Adventist Church must of necessity put his trust wholly and only in the infallible Word of God, whether he be the General Conference President or the newest member of a local congregation. By so doing, individuals have a safeguard that Satan cannot penetrate.

Yes, the men of experience have an important role. It is their responsibility to counsel and guide, not according to their own ideas, but according to the Word of God, asking those who are younger, either in years or in the faith, to consider this or that passage of Scripture or counsel from the servant of the Lord. In so doing, they turn men and women back to God and His Word rather than encouraging them to follow their often-fallible concepts of truth and righteousness.

We would be misleading if we did not point out that we see the same pattern followed a hundred years ago being repeated in the contemporary Seventh-day Adventist Church. We can easily imagine the reaction of the leaders of last century to the following counsel of the Lord, but would we act differently?

> There is manifested on the part of men in responsible positions an unwillingness to confess where they have been in the wrong; and their neglect is working disaster, not only to themselves, but to the churches (*Review and Herald,* Dec. 16, 1890).

If you indulge stubbornness of heart, and through pride and self-righteousness do not confess your faults, you will be left subject to Satan's temptations. If when the Lord reveals your errors you do not repent or make confession, his providence will bring you over the ground again and again. You will be left to make mistakes of a similar character. You will continue to lack wisdom, and will call sin righteousness and righteousness sin. The multitude of deceptions that will prevail in these last days will encircle you and you will change leaders, and not know that you have done so (Ibid., 1890).

By 1894 Sister White was giving even stronger counsel. Surely she wrote the following statement largely because of the leaders' rejection of God's message.

It is a backsliding church that lessens the distance between itself and the papacy (*Signs of the Times,* February 19, 1894).

A little later in the same year, she wrote,

Let us, then, remember that our weakness and inefficiency are largely the results of looking to man, of trusting in man to do those things for us that God has promised to do for those who come unto Him (*Review and Herald,* August 14, 1894).

Even stronger statements followed. By 1895 Sister White had given this sobering message:

The spirit of domination is extending to the presidents of our conferences. If a man is sanguine of his own powers and seeks to exercise dominion over his brethren, feeling that he is invested with authority to make his will the ruling power, the best and only safe course is to remove him, lest great harm be done and he lose his own soul and imperil the souls of others. "All ye are brethren." This disposition to lord it over God's heritage will cause a reaction unless these men change their course. Those in authority should manifest the spirit of Christ. They should deal as He would deal with every case that requires attention. They should go weighted with the Holy Spirit. A man's position does not make him one jot or tittle greater in the sight of God; it is character alone that God values.

The goodness, mercy, and love of God were proclaimed by Christ to Moses. This was God's character. When men who profess to serve God ignore His parental character and depart from honor and righteousness in dealing with their fellowmen, Satan exults, for he has inspired them with his attributes. They are following in the track of Romanism (*Testimonies to Ministers,* page 362).

Finite men should beware of seeking to control their fellowmen, taking the place assigned to the Holy Spirit . . . That which makes me feel to the very depths of my being, and makes me know that their works are not the works of God, is that they suppose they have authority to rule their fellowmen. The Lord has given them no more right to rule others than He has given others to rule them. Those who assume the control of their fellowmen take into their finite hands a work that devolves upon God alone.

That men should keep alive the spirit which ran riot at Minneapolis is an offense to God. All heaven is indignant at the spirit that for years has been revealed in our publishing institution at Battle Creek. Unrighteousness is practiced that God will not tolerate. He will visit for these things (*Testimonies to Ministers,* pages 76-77).

In 1901, Sister White added these words:

There are to be more than one or two or three men to consider the whole vast field. The work is great, and there is no one human mind that can plan for the work which needs to be done (*General Conference Bulletin,* April 3, 1901).

As late as 1909 we have this counsel,

I have been shown that ministers and people are tempted more and more to trust in finite man for wisdom, and to make flesh their arm. To conference presidents, and men in responsible places, I bear this message: Break the bands and fetters that have been placed upon God's people. To you the word is spoken, "Break every yoke." Unless you cease the work of making man amenable to man, unless you become humble in heart, and yourselves learn the way of the Lord as little children, the Lord will divorce you from His work. We are to treat one another as brethren, as fellow laborers, as men and women who are, with us, seeking for light and understanding of the way of the Lord, and who are jealous for His glory (*Testimonies to Ministers,* pages 480-481).

Centralization of power and the increasing domination of leaders over workers, and, in turn, pastors over members, unquestionably have sped the flooding of apostasy into the Seventh-day Adventist Church. God is calling for His people to reorganize according to His pattern, so that the light of truth may be able to shine with all its glory at the end of time. Not only does the Seventh-day Adventist Church need repentance and reformation in the area of truth and righteousness, but it also sorely needs reformation in the area of church administration and authority.

3
Hierarchism

A s we have explored the developmental organization of the church, it has become evident that the organization that God wanted for His church was the antithesis of hierarchicalism. God chose a representative government for the orderly prosecution of the gospel commission. In his book, *The Supremacy of Peter* (Review and Herald, 1898), M. E. Kellogg brought these issues into clear focus by showing the error of the papal system and expounding the system of the New Testament which brought great reward to God's people. He explained the situation as follows:

> It has been proved in the preceding chapters that the idea of a primacy is unknown in the Scriptures, and that the primacy which was established, was only accomplished by unholy ambition and an unchristian seeking for spiritual supremacy, entirely foreign to the spirit and teachings of Christ and His apostles; we have also seen that it was accomplished after long centuries of plotting and scheming, and especially by the union of this then-apostate church with the Roman state, and that it finally resulted in bringing the Roman state and many other states under the control of the church; that a large part of the Christian church always protested against it; and that the separation between the churches of the East and the West in the eleventh century was to some extent over this question; for the Eastern Church never accepted the supremacy of the bishop of Rome. Since that time numerous bodies of Christians have denied the doctrine of the primacy. The great reformers of the sixteenth century made the denial of the primacy a cardinal feature of their work, and it is held by none but by the Roman Catholic Church. This church firmly maintains this doctrine as a fundamental portion of its creed (M. E. Kellogg, *The Supremacy of Peter*, pp. 259, 260).

In further commenting upon this, M. E. Kellogg said,

> There is to be no primacy. The gospel is designed for all the world. Churches are to be raised everywhere, but there is no provision in the Christian system whereby one man, or a

conclave of men in continual session, is to take the charge of the work of the gospel in all the world. Such a task would be entirely beyond the capacity of man. The world is large; and the idea that one man, or one body of men, could take into consideration the spiritual needs of all believers in Christ, or the spiritual needs of many thousands of believers in Christ, which are scattered throughout the world, is preposterous (Ibid., p. 260).

It has been a great grief to many Seventh-day Adventists that leaders of the Seventh-day Adventist Church, in two well-publicized court cases, have argued from the perspective of a hierarchic structure in their endeavor to win the favorable decision of the court. This happened in the Merikay Silver case in California in her suit against Pacific Press in the 1970's, and again in the Derek Proctor (an Andrews University professor) case in his suit against the General Conference. Here is a summary of the Proctor case.

> Dr. Derek Proctor's long-running lawsuit with the Seventh-day Adventist Church was finally decided on October 29, 1986. Proctor lost the case, in which he contended that the church in various of its entities conspired illegally to interfere in his book-selling business in violation of anti-trust and conspiracy laws. The major strategy of the General Conference in this case was to convince the court that the Seventh-day Adventist Church is essentially an hierarchical church, in which the directives and orders of the General Conference have binding authority upon all other entities of the church. The General Conference submitted that, "next to the Roman Catholic Church, the Adventist Church is the most centralized of all major Christian denominations in this country" (*Student Movement*—Student paper of Andrews University, November 6, 1986).

The central theme of the Merikay case is as follows:

> Although it is true that there was a period in the life of the Seventh-day Adventist Church when the denomination took a distinctly anti-Roman Catholic viewpoint, and the term "hierarchy" was used in a pejorative sense to refer to the papal form of the church governance, that attitude on the church's part was nothing more than a manifestation of widespread

anti-popery among conservative Protestant denominations in the early part of this century, and the latter part of the last, which has now been consigned to the historical trash heap as far as the Seventh-day Adventist Church is concerned (sworn affidavit of Neal C. Wilson, Vice President of the General Conference of Seventh-day Adventists—in the Merikay McLeod lawsuit: Page 4, Footnote #2, Docket entry #84: EEOC vs. PPPA, C-74-2025-CBR. February 6, 1976).

Surely it is with horror that we look at this drift toward hierarchism in God's remnant church. As we explained earlier, the hierarchal form of government is the claimed prerogative of the Roman Catholic Church; it is the papal form of governance designed by Satan to centralize power in one individual, or at the most, a few individuals, so that he (they) might have a greater opportunity to control other individuals, thus derailing the direction of the church.

It will be noticed that in the Proctor case the declaration very clearly suggests that the church members are expected to follow the binding decisions of the General Conference. There are only two explanations to such a claim. Either it represented perjury in that it was a deliberate misrepresentation of the facts, or as a church we have renounced the God-given principles of divine organization for this church.

Some have referred to the calling together of the church council in the fifteenth chapter of Acts, and have suggested that this presupposes a hierarchal organization; such is not the case. From the context of the Biblical record it will be seen that the calling of the Jerusalem Council was rather an ad hoc committee, not a standing committee.

And the apostles and elders came together for to consider of this matter (Acts 15:6).

We do not know how James was chosen to give the summary report. Some have referred to him as the "General Conference president," but that would hardly be accurate from the context. It is very likely that he was chosen by the group of apostles and elders to chair the meeting, or perhaps to be the one to declare the final decision after prayerful seeking of the answers that God had given to them.

Commenting upon this council, M. E. Kellogg wrote,

The thing nearest to universal authority and headship in the church is the action of a general council. The 15th chapter of the Acts of the Apostles will ever stand as unmistakable evidence that the measure of authority, which primarily belongs to the church as a whole, is, at special times, and for certain definite purposes, vested in a council; that the council may be summoned whenever great questions arise that threaten division in the church, or at regular intervals if necessary, for the consideration of questions which affect the interests of the whole church; and that the decisions of the councils so convened, are advisory rather than actually obligatory on the church. Stated broadly, actual legislative power is not committed to the church. All actual legislation was done by Christ (M. E. Kellogg, Op. Cit., pp. 261, 262).

Kellogg gave further clarification,

A Christian council is a convention for a limited space of time. When it is in actual session, it is the repository of all the authority there is in the church, and therefore its decisions should not be lightly regarded. But when a council is disbanded, the general and advisory power vested therein is for the time suspended until the next council; and there is no provision in the Christian system of church government by which the authority of the general and universal council may be transferred to any one who shall represent the council between its sessions, and thus form a general and continuous head to the church on earth. This would be an usurpation of the place of Christ, the only true head of the church.

Continuous and general authority over the whole church by men, involves a responsibility so great that God, in His infinite wisdom and mercy, thought it not best that it be committed to a man or men (Ibid. pp. 262, 263).

However, the very problem that M. E. Kellogg was addressing in the Roman Catholic Church is now more than a little evident in the Seventh-day Adventist Church. Kellogg further warned,

What, then, is necessary to constitute an earthly head, a master of the church? Not so much, perhaps, as many people imagine. Stated in a simple manner, to possess an earthly head, a church needs but to have one man, or one body of men, constantly taking the oversight of the work of the church in all parts of the world alike. This will generally necessitate a permanent and central place for frequent conference and consultation; the communication to this body of the state of the different portions of the church in every part of the world where this church has any organization; and the consideration of the same with directions and commands to the church everywhere. When a church has this, it has, as far as the headship is concerned, though it may be upon a smaller scale, a miniature of that first headship located on the Tiber—it has that for which there is no warrant in the Scriptures.

The churches of Jesus Christ, in any and every country, must have organization, and men should be elected by free vote of the members to take the oversight of the affairs of the church; but these men would be heads only for a limited time over a small portion of the church. The men elected would be quite well known, probably personally known to all. They would not be removed from those who gave them their temporary authority by an exaggerated height of excellence or knowledge, and hence any attempt by them to exert an unauthorized and arbitrary power would be quickly checked by the body of the church, which is the superior authority and final arbiter in all matters pertaining to itself (Ibid., pp. 263, 264).

What a wonderful thing it would be if we were to follow more closely the governance form as set out here by Kellogg! It will be noted that the superior authority and the final arbiter, according to Kellogg, is the body of the church itself. This is the basis of the representative form of church governance. It is the basis of the inverted pyramidal structure that God gave to this church. Today, however, we see a striking hierarchal form developing, which is a curse to Christianity, and is a dishonor to God, Who alone has the responsibility of leadership in the church.

In commenting upon the hierarchal form, Kellogg further said,

The gospel plan is a better way than this; it allows a greater degree of freedom and independence to the members of the church, and also provides for such concentration of effort as will carry the gospel to the world, and furnish pastoral care to the churches already established. This may be seen by referring to the Acts of the Apostles.

As the apostles went forth proclaiming the gospel, churches were raised; and after these had been sufficiently proved and elders had been ordained in every city (Titus 1:5), these churches took their places as independent parts of the church of Christ. Not that they were independent of the advisory power of the general council, if anything among them needed to be considered by that body upon its convention, but aside from that they were independent. These churches would naturally form into associations for mutual council and cooperation, but in them there existed no arbitrary authority more than exists in every separate church for the correction and discipline of its members (ibid., pp. 265, 266).

The rulership of one man or a small group of men over other men and women is not very different from the mind-control programs that Sister White condemned. With all honesty, we must admit that this rulership is increasingly happening on a dangerously large scale today. Where men are unable to move ahead on their own, for fear they may call forth the displeasure of someone who is considered to be in a higher position in God's work, the work is hindered. This interference must not be the case. The Lord in His wisdom gave counsel comparing the Christian order with the pagan order. These statements came after the terrible anger expressed by ten disciples over the request of the mother of John and James, who asked for Jesus to grant preeminence to her sons in Christ's kingdom. Jesus realized that He needed to solve this dispute, and He did so with these words:

And Jesus called them unto him, and said, Ye know that the princes of the Gentiles exercise dominion over them, and they that are great exercise authority upon them. But it shall not be so among you: but whosoever will be great among you, let him be your minister; and whosoever will be chief among you, let him be your servant: even as the Son of man came not to be ministered unto, but to minister, and to give his life a ransom for many (Matthew 20:25-28).

It is worldly practice to have hierarchical structures and authoritative leaders. It is not acceptable practice to Christianity. God has called for leaders who are servants and ministers: those who will counsel and guide, not rule and dominate. The Lord has spoken strongly on this matter.

Those whom God has placed in positions of responsibility should never seek to exalt themselves or to turn the attention of men to their work. They must give all the glory to God. They must not seek for power that they may lord it over God's heritage; for only those who are under the rule of Satan will do this.

But the rule-or-ruin system is too often seen in our institutions. This spirit is cherished and revealed by some in responsible positions, and because of this God cannot do the work He desires to do through them. By their course of action those who reveal this spirit make manifest what they would be in heaven if entrusted with responsibility (*Testimonies to Ministers,* pp. 279, 280).

Let no plans or methods be adopted in any of our institutions that will bind mind or talent under the control of human judgment; for this is not in God's order. God has given to men talents of influence which belong to Him alone, and no greater dishonor can be done to God than for one finite agent to bring other men's talent under his absolute control, even though the benefits of the same be used to the advantage of the cause. In such arrangements one man's mind is ruled by another man's mind, and the human agency is separated from God and exposed to temptation. Satan's method tends to one end—to make men the slaves of men. And when this is done, confusion and distrust, jealousies and evil surmisings, are the result. Such a course destroys faith in God and in the principles which are to control, to purge from guile and every species of selfishness and hypocrisy (Ibid., pp. 360, 361).

Taking it up from another perspective, the servant of the Lord had this to say,

The conferences are watching every move made at the center of the work. The different conferences have been led to look to leading men at Battle Creek, feeling that no important move can be made without their approval. This tendency has been growing stronger, until it is a serious hindrance to the advancement of the work. This arrangement should never have been. The Lord would have His people under His jurisdiction. They should look to God, inquiring of Him in faith, and follow on to know the working of His providence (Ibid., p. 321).

Sister White saw that the leaders of the work should not always be ministers. In fact, it seems that sometimes she favored laymen being chosen for these positions.

> In each country a man should be appointed to work in the general interests of the cause. He need not be a preacher, and he must not be a policy man. He should be unselfish, a man who loves, who honors, and fears his God. His whole time should be devoted to the work. He should plan unselfishly, and in the fear of God. Let him be general agent for that country, and let him be connected with a council composed of the very best men, that they may counsel together, and attend to the work within their borders (Ibid., p. 321).

> The danger of one man controlling another, or indeed, one man looking to another as his guide and controller, has fearful consequences in terms of the Judgment. Therefore, the divine counsel is to break every such yoke.

> I write thus fully, because I have been shown that ministers and people are tempted more and more to trust in finite man for wisdom, and to make flesh their arm. To conference presidents, and men in responsible places, I bear this message: Break the bands and fetters that have been placed upon God's people. To you the word is spoken, "Break every yoke." Unless you cease the work of making man amenable to man, unless you become humble in heart, and yourselves learn the way of the Lord as little children, the Lord will divorce you from His work. We are to treat one another as brethren, as fellow laborers, as men and women who are, with us, seeking for light and understanding of the way of the Lord, and who are jealous for His glory (Ibid., pp 480, 481).

The role of leaders is never to rule, to dictate, or to control. They are to counsel and advise. Again the servant of the Lord speaks:

> Men whom the Lord calls to important positions in His work are to cultivate a humble dependence upon Him. They are not to seek to embrace too much authority; for God has not called them to a work of ruling, but to plan and counsel with their fellow laborers. Every worker alike is to hold himself amenable to the requirements and instructions of God (*Testimonies for the Church*, Volume 9, p. 270).

Today we not only have much rulership in our church, but we also have clear indications that such is the official direction of our church. The Spirit of God cannot be poured out upon His people, and leaders cannot achieve under God what they might, if they have chosen the pathway of the pagans rather than the pathway of God. Furthermore, when men submit to such ungodly rulership, they themselves are culpable because of what they have done. God has called us to counsel together, but never to be controlled by other human beings. Such control short-circuits the relationship that should exist only between God and man.

Gary Krause, Associate Editor of the *South Pacific Record*, wrote a perceptive and troubling item in his editorial after the 1990 General Conference Session. The editorial, entitled "View From a FAX Machine," had this to say:

> The session has demonstrated the hierarchal nature of the church's administrative structure. Of course, there is nothing intrinsically wrong with such a system. [The authors of this book strongly disagree.] In fact, it has advantages. But there is potential trouble when we start viewing various offices within that system as "more prestigious" than others or, to use George Orwell's phrase, "more equal than others."

> The problem is that a hierarchical system suggests a ladder of importance from GC down to local church. It implies that transferring from church pastor to an administrative position is "a move up the ladder," while this vice versa is a "demotion."

> And a hierarchal system also makes it easier for a lot of attention to focus on the president of that system. But even this is *not necessarily* a problem.

> However, it does raise questions of perspective when the General Conference president is repeatedly referred to as "President Folkenberg." And when an Adventist refers to Mrs. Folkenberg as the Seventh-day Adventist Church's "FIRST LADY," it makes you wonder. It probably has the same effect on Mrs. Folkenberg, who appears to be a particularly self-effacing, humble woman (*South Pacific Record,* August 4, 1990, p. 2).

The evidence is gaining momentum and is too strong to be ignored. The Seventh-day Adventist Church is following the hierarchal pattern of the Roman Catholic Church. It is time for a mighty reformation. Laity and ministry alike need to earnestly work together to reverse this most dangerous situation.

4

The Ecumenical Trap

The ecumenical movement is a device of Satan in his wicked attempt to bring the whole world under his control. This movement makes recourse to the words of Jesus in His prayer for unity in John seventeen. Especially do its leaders focus upon that beautiful verse which pleads:

> That they all may be one; as thou, Father, art in me, and I in thee, that they also may be one in us: that the world may believe that thou hast sent me (John 17:21).

However, they never search for the vital formula for such unity, which is found in the seventeenth verse.

> Sanctify them through thy truth: thy word is truth (John 17:17).

This key is confirmed a little later in the prayer,

> And for their sakes I sanctify myself, that they also might be sanctified through the truth (John 17:19).

In the cursory study of this unity prayer, ecumenical leaders have failed to concentrate on the issues of truth and righteousness. The ecumenical movement is predicated upon a deemphasizing of truth and doctrine, and a claim to call everyone into the love of God. However, such is the call of Satan, and is based upon spiritualism, when not presented in the context of truth and righteousness.

> Spiritualism is now changing its form, veiling some of its more objectionable and immoral features, and assuming a Christian guise. Formerly it denounced Christ and the Bible; now it professes to accept both. The Bible is interpreted in a manner that is attractive to the unrenewed heart, while its solemn and vital truths are made of no effect. *A God of love is presented; but His justice, His denunciation of sin, the requirements of His holy law, are all kept out of sight. Pleasing, bewitching fables captivate the senses of those who do not make God's Word the foundation of their faith. Christ is*

*as verily rejected as before; but Satan has so blinded the eyes
of the people that the deception is not discerned (Spirit of
Prophecy,* Volume 4, p. 405, emphasis added).

Those supporting the ecumenical movement clearly call for a
de-emphasis of doctrine.

We realize that deep theological differences have separated
these three branches of Christendom for centuries. Thus we
must compromise. We have to set aside our theological differences and draw up a common statement of faith (*Proposal
For A Joint Worldwide Movement,* by Robert Meyers, p. 17).

The things that separate us cannot be the issue. Theological
differences will have to be set aside. The main issue is the
truth that we find in the Bible and the creeds, which we agree
upon. As we get to know one another better, theological differences can more easily be addressed (Ibid., p. 19).

Issues not to be addressed would include Calvinism versus
Arminian doctrine, Biblical inerrancy, predestination, modes of
baptism, whether the Holy Spirit comes from the Father alone or
the Father and the Son (Filioque), pre-, post-, or a-millennialism,
glossolalia, whether or not the pope is infallible and is the sole
head of the church, ordination of women, Saturday or Sunday
worship, the place of Mary in our faith, the dating of Easter, the
number of sacraments, eternal security, whether the Lord's Supper is symbolic, consubstantial (the host representing the spiritual
presence of Christ), or transubstantial (the host actually becoming
the body and blood of Christ), and other issues (Ibid, p. 19).

Indeed, the de-emphasizing of doctrine is the basis of the
major thrust of the World Council of Churches. Meeting in Lima,
Peru, in January of 1982, more than 100 theologians voted what
is known as the BEM Document—Baptism, Eucharist and Ministry. Ever since, de-emphasis has become perhaps the major thrust
of the World Council of Churches as it tries to draw the many
churches into agreement with this document. In brief, the BEM
Document calls for the following:

1. Baptism: no discrimination is to be made about the mode of
baptism or the way of baptizing.

When we consider that there were many who were martyred because of their stand for biblical baptism by immersion, no true Seventh-day Adventist could ever agree to such.

2. Eucharist, the Catholic term for the communion service.

Again the call is that there be no difference or distinction made between the various beliefs concerning the communion. Roman Catholics believe that the wafer is the very body of Christ, and in blasphemy they claim that the priest holds Christ in his hand and, as it were, he becomes the creator of his Creator. Hardly could true Adventists agree with such, and yet today we find in some Adventist churches the word *Eucharist* is used in preference to *communion*. This practice is devastating to any perceptive Seventh-day Adventist.

3. Ministering. The concept is that no church will proselytize members of another church; we will all seek to proselytize only the unchurched. This concept is antithetic to the final call of the last cry of Revelation 18,

> Come out of her, my people, that ye be not partakers of her sins, and that ye receive not of her plagues (Revelation 18:4).

Perhaps the most devastating aspect of this document is the claim on the back of the BEM document that the vote to transmit this agreed statement was an unanimous vote, and the Seventh-day Adventist Church is listed among those represented.

One thing is certain, the Adventist delegate did not vote against such a wholly Satan-inspired document. This document has been presented to over 170 churches for their responses.

The drifts toward ecumenism in the Seventh-day Adventist Church are frighteningly rampant. In the confines of this book it would be impossible to list the myriad of evidences that we are inextricably binding ourselves to this end-time deception of Satan. Let us look at a few of the evidences.

1. **Non-distinctive sermons.** The testimony of numerous Seventh-day Adventists is that their pastors are no longer preaching the distinctive message of the three angels. They are no longer presenting the pillars of the Advent faith. Many sermons, not neces-

sarily false, but containing nothing of present truth, are being presented. As one man reported, his pastor preaches "pleasant truth." That is wholly unacceptable at the end of time. The servant of the Lord declared that it is possible for Satan to gain every advantage if we preach precious truth but ignore present truth. This situation has been a tremendous challenge over many years for the authors of this book. Sister White warned us,

> There are many precious truths contained in the Word of God, but it is "*present truth*" that the flock needs now. I have seen the danger of the messengers running off from the important points of present truth, to dwell upon subjects that are not calculated to unite the flock and sanctify the soul. *Satan will here take every possible advantage to injure the cause.*
>
> But such subjects as the sanctuary, in connection with the 2300 days, the commandments of God and the faith of Jesus, are perfectly calculated to explain the past Advent movement and show what our present position is, establish the faith of the doubting, and give certainty to the glorious future. These, I have frequently seen, were the principal subjects on which the messenger should dwell (*Early Writings,* p. 63, emphasis added).

It is not necessary to preach error for Satan to gain an advantage. We ask the reader, Have you recently heard from the pulpit of your church a sermon on the sanctuary, the state of the dead, the Investigative Judgment, the Sabbath, or even upon the imminent return of Jesus Christ? If you can say yes to all or even most of these, you are blessed with a pastor who loves the Lord, loves this truth, and knows the way of God. But we are convinced that most of you, sadly, will have to say that it has been many, many years since you have heard such a message. Too many laity are satisfied to hear messages that contain no overt error, and may even rejoice that at least their pastor is not preaching falsehood. In some cases such pastors are far more dangerous, for it is much more difficult to point out the hazard in such circumstances.

2. **Ministerial fraternals.** Many of our ministers have joined the community ministerial fraternal, a fellowship of ministers of various faiths in each community. Indeed, in many instances they are

encouraged to do so. It is falsely believed that union with the ministerial fraternals will provide a greater opportunity to witness to the ministers of other faiths. Certainly Sister White has given Seventh-day Adventist ministers a very important challenge to witness to ministers of other denominations. However, joining them in their fellowship is an entirely different situation. Once we have befriended and been befriended by these other ministers, it is much more difficult to openly proselytize members of their churches. The pastor feels the pressure because of the embarrassment it would cause if he were to win a soul from the church of one of the fraternal members. We know of specific cases where ministers have refused to proselytize because of this very situation. Beware of any minister, or indeed any Seventh-day Adventist, who keeps emphasizing that we must work for the unchurched. We must certainly work for the unchurched, but probably the implication is that we should not work for those of another faith. The call of Christ is,

> Come out of her, my people, that ye be not partakers of her sins, and that ye receive not of her plagues (Revelation 18:4).

3. **The exchange of pulpits.** Closely associated with the ministerial fraternal has been the increasing incidence of Seventh-day Adventist pastors exchanging pulpits with pastors of other faiths. This is a major ecumenical step. Of course, it may start very innocently. The pastor of a church of another denomination might open-heartedly invite a Seventh-day Adventist pastor to preach in his church. However, often the expectation is that the Seventh-day Adventist pastor will request the pastor of the other faith to preach in his church. This is taking place to the point that we have even had Roman Catholics preaching in our pulpits, as well as many ministers of other Protestant denominations. How can such feed the flock with present truth? It is essential that the pulpits of the Seventh-day Adventist Church be kept for those who love and preach the truth. The confusion that exists with many of our laity is that while those not of our faith are readily able to gain access to our pulpits in certain areas, usually the same pulpits are not available to those who truly preach the end-time three angels' messages.

4. The loss of the identification of the antichrist. Again we might ask the question, How long since you have heard from the pulpit of your church the identification of the Roman Catholic Church as the antichrist, as the man of sin, as the little horn, as the beast power of Babylon, as the immoral woman, et cetera? These identifications are being lost, until often the antichrist is identified in general terms as those who do not worship Christ, the pagan world, and so forth. The Reformation was built upon a clear identification of the Roman Catholic Church as the antichrist, and so was the Seventh-day Adventist Church. This is not intended to lead to strife and hostility; however, we must know who the antichrist is, so that we can call men and women out of Babylon into the glorious light of the three angels' messages, that they may prepare their lives for the return of Jesus Christ.

5. Easter sunrise sermon. We do not believe we need to explain the pagan origin of the Easter sunrise service. An examination of Ezekiel, chapter eight gives a clear picture of how God abhors this worship of the sunrise. Everything about the Easter sunrise service is pagan; it is, quite simply, the worship of the rising sun. While it may be held that Easter takes place about the time of the Passover, when Jesus was crucified, any knowledgeable Christian is fully aware that the Easter services arose from paganism. Frequently, Seventh-day Adventists play a major role in these sunrise services, and have been reported in many parts of the world in a positive light because of it. However, true Seventh-day Adventists could never participate in such a service. Often the services are of an ecumenical nature, and even if they are not, they represent another thrust toward the ecumenical development within the Seventh-day Adventist Church.

6. The observer status at the World Council of Churches. It is true that the Seventh-day Adventist Church is not an official member of the World Council of Churches. Nevertheless, it would seem that we are participating more frequently in the so-called observer role, and it is obvious that we are being slowly drawn into this movement which comes from the evil mind of Satan.

Wisdom dictates that we should withdraw from any association with this organization, which is designed to bring all of Christendom under the banner of the papacy.

7. **Official observers at the General Conference Sessions.** For the last several General Conference Sessions, we have been inviting leaders of other churches to offer their greetings, sometimes their prayers and liturgies, for the success of the session. The consternation of faithful Adventists reached a climax in 1990 when Thomas Murphy, the Director for Ecumenical Affairs at the Archdiocese of Indianapolis, offered his greetings at the session as an official observer, and also prayed a liturgical prayer for the success of the conference. Words cannot describe the heart-rending burden that such an irresponsible act brought to the hearts of every faithful Seventh-day Adventist lay member or minister. Surely each faithful member has been calling in clear terms for reversal of this approach at the next General Conference Session. We do not need the blessing nor the prayers of those who do not understand the message for this time. We need the guidance and blessing of the God of heaven alone.

8. **Affiliation with New Age organizations.** Many Seventh-day Adventists in Australia have been burdened that in recent years the Ingathering brochure has indicated that ADRA is affiliated with the ACFOA (Australian Council for Overseas Aid). This is a New Age organization that is helping to orchestrate the movement for a one-world government. We ask with pained hearts, How can even a few leaders in our church be so blind and irresponsible as to make such an affiliation? Was it done in ignorance, or full knowledge? If it was done in full knowledge, it represents a denial of our Lord. If it was done in ignorance, those responsible are hardly less culpable, for surely it is important to discover with whom we are in league.

> Be ye not unequally yoked together with unbelievers: for what fellowship hath righteousness with unrighteousness? and what communion hath light with darkness? And what concord hath Christ with Belial? or what part hath he that believeth with an infidel? And what agreement hath the temple of God with idols? for ye are the temple of the living God; as God hath

said, I will dwell in them, and walk in them; and I will be their God, and they shall be my people. Wherefore come out from among them, and be ye separate, saith the Lord, and touch not the unclean thing; and I will receive you (2 Corinthians 6:14-17).

Here is the call that God is making to His people today. We must remove ourselves from every association with the ecumenical movement.

5
The Church or the Word

From 1909 to 1915, the Seventh-day Adventist Church published a very important magazine called *Protestant Magazine*. W. W. Prescott, the first educational director of the General Conference, edited it. Its associate editors were F. C. Wilcox, Editor of the *Review and Herald*, and W. A. Spicer, then secretary, later to become president of the General Conference. These fine statements, "Advocating Primitive Christianity" and "Protesting Against Apostasy," appeared on the front page of each issue of the magazine. Each issue also had a different statement concerning Protestantism on its front cover. In its September, 1914 issue, under the title, "A Vital Difference," it made this dramatic statement: "Protestantism makes the relation of the individual to the church dependent on his relation to Christ; Catholicism, vice versa, makes the relation of the individual to Christ dependent on his relation to the church." This principle is just as fundamental today as it has ever been. The Protestant Reformation was built upon the primacy of the Word.

The Advent Movement began because Protestants were withdrawing from the Word and holding to ecclesiastical principles independent of the Word. This was certainly true in relationship to the law of God, and especially to the fourth commandment. However, it was also true in the area of the state of the dead and the issue of baptism. When our pioneers took the fuller light of the Advent Message to these churches, they discovered that these churches held to a "thus saith the church" much more strongly than a "thus saith the Word." Today, the Seventh-day Adventist Church faces this same threat.

Truth is not eclectic; truth is not pluralistic. It cannot be, for truth is absolute, riveted in the eternal character of God Himself. Nevertheless, we see many Seventh-day Adventists proclaiming the dangerous ecumenical theme of unity in diversity. Many are boldly proclaiming their adherence to pluralistic principles, but God cannot lie (Titus 1:2, Numbers 23:19); Jesus is the Truth

(John 14:6). On the other side, Satan is the father of lies (John 8:44). Thus, eclecticism and pluralism always have their roots in error.

When we move one step away from revealed truth, we stand on Satan's territory. It does not matter how much truth something has in it. If we have a minute amount of error, we have a philosophy riveted in the deceptions of Satan. A principle with a minute amount of error contained in it cannot be from God any more than water can remain pure if someone places a couple of drops of strychnine in it. There is only one truth. There are unlimited numbers of errors. Satan uses all kinds of errors to deceive mankind, and he can effectively use any mixture of truth and error. One of the most dangerous concepts heard within Adventism today is, There is a lot of truth in it. It is implied that there is also error, and that makes the concept Satan's deception. The Word of God stresses the fact that we cannot depend upon man, whether it be our own human wisdom or the human wisdom of others.

It is not in man that walketh to direct his steps (Jeremiah 10:23).

Thus saith the Lord; Cursed be the man that trusteth in man, and maketh flesh his arm, and whose heart departeth from the Lord (Jeremiah 17:5).

The only unqualified trust must be in the Lord and His Word.

Blessed is that man that maketh the Lord his trust, and respecteth not the proud, nor such as turn aside to lies (Psalm 40:4).

It is better to trust in the Lord than to put confidence in man (Psalm 118:8).

Thy word is a lamp unto my feet, and a light unto my path (Psalm 119:105).

Trust in the Lord with all thine heart; and lean not unto thine own understanding. In all thy ways acknowledge him, and he shall direct thy paths (Proverbs 3:5, 6).

A man's heart deviseth his way: but the Lord directeth his steps (Proverbs 16:9).

Let us hear the conclusion of the whole matter: Fear God, and keep his commandments: for this is the whole duty of man (Ecclesiastes 12:13).

We are deeply concerned as we observe more and more men and women leaning upon the counsel of men in leadership rather than following the direct counsel of God. Of course, there must be a significant level of loyalty and respect for human leaders; nevertheless, that loyalty and respect must never supersede the primary loyalty that we owe to God. Men are often asked to affirm their loyalty to the church, but the call to affirm our loyalty to Christ and to His Word is rare.

Frequently, when the call to affirm loyalty to the church is made, the unspoken call is for loyalty to leaders, irrespective of their faithfulness or unfaithfulness to the Word of God. Loyalty to man can never be absolute in the same way that loyalty to God must be. God cannot accept calls of loyalty to the church if they are not predicated upon our loyalty to Christ. When Christ had to make a choice between the truth of God and the church of God, He always chose the truth of God. Because of it, the leaders of the church killed him.

In commenting upon authority of church leaders down through the ages, the servant of the Lord said,

> The only condition upon which the freedom of man is possible is that of becoming one with Christ. "The truth shall make you free;" and Christ is the truth. Sin can triumph only by enfeebling the mind and destroying the liberty of the soul. Subjection to God is restoration to one's self—to the true glory and dignity of man. The divine law, to which we are brought into subjection, is "the law of liberty" (James 2:12).

> The Pharisees had declared themselves the children of Abraham. Jesus told them that this claim could be established only by doing the works of Abraham. The true children of Abraham would live, as he did, a life of obedience to God. They would not try to kill One who was speaking the truth that was given Him from God. In plotting against Christ, the rabbis were not doing the works of Abraham. A mere lineal descent from Abraham was of no value. Without a spiritual

connection with Him, which would be manifested in possessing the same spirit, and doing the same works, they were not his children.

This principle bears with equal weight upon a question that has long agitated the Christian world—the question of apostolic succession. Descent from Abraham was proved, not by name and lineage, but by likeness of character. So the apostolic succession rests not upon the transmission of ecclesiastical authority, but upon spiritual relationship. A life actuated by the apostles' spirit, the belief and teaching of the truth they taught, this is the true evidence of apostolic succession. This is what constitutes men the successors of the first teachers of the gospel (*The Desire of Ages,* pages 466–467).

Unfortunately, evidence is now accumulating that in God's remnant church there are increasing calls for loyalty to the church, which is not predicated upon loyalty to Christ and His Word. Toward the end of 1991, a letter sent out by the pastor and church elder of the Bury-St. Edmonds Seventh-day Adventist Company in Britain accentuated this misdirected loyalty. His letter called for a number of faithful Adventists to sign a document affirming their loyalty to a number of propositions. These included,

> I promise to give my loyalty and support to the best of my ability to all the meetings of the church including the prayer meeting.

> I promise to work in cooperation with the officers in the church instead of doing an independent ministry that is often divisive.

> I promise to distribute only authorized church materials to new contacts in the church.

> I promise not to send out invitations to meetings that have not been approved of by the church.

Such promises should never be asked. While each member truly has a responsibility to be loyal to the church, sometimes members may have to express their loyalty by opposing directions within the church that are not consistent with the Word of God. Often the less faithful members evaluate these members, who express their loyalty by upholding truth and righteousness, as divisive and schismatic. However, every faithful Adventist must oppose error and uphold God's Word if he will stand clear in the judgment.

As youngsters growing up in the Seventh-day Adventist Church, we heard frequently, "We have no creed but the Bible." "The Bible and the Bible only is our basis of faith and practice." This is what set the Seventh-day Adventist Church apart from all other churches. It was the basis upon which we rejected Catholicism and those forms of apostate Protestantism that had deviated from the pure, clear testimony of God's Word. True Adventism still stands on this foundation. The Seventh-day Adventist Church has no reason to exist unless it remains built upon the unadulterated truths and principles of divine inspiration. To move away from these places the Seventh-day Adventist Church on the same platform as the Roman Catholic Church and the fallen churches of Protestantism.

God is calling for a people who will stand loyal to Him in this time of disloyalty. It is often easier to stand loyal to God when dealing with those not of our faith, rather than when reasoning with our own Seventh-day Adventist brethren; nevertheless, we must remain steadfast in the face of opposition from those within the church who deviate from the doctrines of the Word. Only thus can we prepare to meet our Lord when He comes.

6

Adventist, Not Evangelical

The alarming drift of many within the Seventh-day Adventist Church toward the evangelical approach to theology has devastated and deeply burdened faithful members of the church. While unquestionably the roots of this apostasy go back into earlier Adventist history, the events that took place in the mid-1950s were obviously the basis upon which the movement gained enormous emphasis. The situation started innocently. On one occasion the then-president of the East Pennsylvania Conference, Elder D. E. Unruh, had been impressed by a sermon presented by Dr. Donald Barnhouse. Dr. Barnhouse was the pastor of the Tenth Presbyterian Church in Philadelphia and was also a most prominent Evangelical and the editor of the well-supported *Eternity* magazine. So impressed was Elder Unruh that he wrote a letter of appreciation to Dr. Barnhouse. As can be well understood, Dr. Barnhouse was not a little surprised to receive such appreciation from a Seventh-day Adventist minister, especially a conference president.

It was not long after this that Walter Martin, having decided to write his doctoral thesis on the cults, enlisted the help of Dr. Barnhouse in his project. Very fairly, they decided that they should not depend upon what others had written about the churches. They decided to approach leaders and authentic representatives of the respective churches to answer questions which they would address to them. When dealing with the Seventh-day Adventist Church, Dr. Barnhouse recalled the letter that he had received from Elder Unruh. He contacted Elder Unruh and placed before him the request that representative leaders of the Seventh-day Adventist Church prepare authoritative answers to their prepared questions.

Impressed, Elder Unruh contacted Elder Reuben Figuhr, the president of the General Conference, enlisting his help. Elder Figuhr replied favorably, and a small group of principals was chosen to meet with Dr. Barnhouse and Walter Martin to answer the many questions posed. The committee consisted of Elders LeRoy Froom, General Conference Field Secretary; R. Allan Anderson, Ministerial Secretary of the General Conference; W. E. Reed, General Conference Field Secretary; and F. D. Nichol, Editor of the *Review and Herald.* For reasons not altogether clear, Elder Nichol faded out of the picture very quickly. Some have suggested it was because of his disagreement with the answers agreed upon by Elders Froom, Anderson, and Reed, but we have not confirmed this.

Out of the answers that were presented, the book *Seventh-day Adventists Answer Questions on Doctrine* developed. Here the world Seventh-day Adventist Church had the opportunity to learn what answers had been given to the Evangelical questioners by these leaders. The book, subsidized by the denomination, was scattered like the leaves of autumn. Most Adventists eagerly sought the book because they felt it represented the first "official" systematic statement of the beliefs of the Seventh-day Adventist Church. However, it was not long before those of deep commitment to the Adventist faith sensed that in this book there had been a tragic betrayal of the true Adventist message.

On the other hand, the book had received a very favorable response from Dr. Barnhouse and Walter Martin. For example, Dr. Barnhouse wrote,

> I should like to say that we are delighted to do justice to a much-maligned group of sincere believers, and in our minds and hearts take them out of a group of other heretics to acknowledge them as redeemed brethren and members of the body of Christ (*Eternity,* September 1, 1956).

This statement was startling when one considers that not much more than six years before Dr. Barnhouse had so aggressively condemned the beautiful book, *Steps to Christ.* In this condemnation he had said that the book contained "half-truths and Satanic error" (*Eternity,* June, 1950). It was clear that this man, who also in the same article referred to Sister White as the founder of a cult, had greatly changed his opinion. No doubt this dramatic change was the result of answers that had been given by the chosen representatives of the General Conference. We hasten to add that about two hundred leaders around the world had also reviewed the questions and answers before the book *Questions on Doctrine* was published. Not a few of these leaders later confessed that because of their busy schedules they scarcely had time to do more than scan the material. This fact had tragic consequences. It is likely that far more theologians than administrators and evangelists found time to read the manuscript with care. Thus those most likely to detect error were the least likely to have read the manuscript in detail.

To the ordinary Seventh-day Adventist minister and lay person the changes were alarming. We were young men in our early- to mid-twenties at this time. Though we did not understand what was taking place, we did feel a great degree of alarm.

We were studying at the University of Sydney. Russell shared his concerns with Colin relating what he had heard at the divine service of the Wahroonga Church (headquarters of the South Pacific Division) in Sydney the previous Sabbath. The secretary (later president) of the Australasian Division, Pastor Lawrence C. Naden, had explained during that church service the "wonderful event" that had taken place in the United States where the Evangelicals were now prepared to accept the Seventh-day Adventist Church as part of the body of Christ and to declare that they no longer considered the Seventh-day Adventist Church to be a cult. Instinctively Russell, although only twenty-three years old at the time, felt there had to be something wrong. When the fallen churches of Babylon gave such a favorable approval to the Seventh-day Adventist Church, some misrepresentation must have taken place. When he shared his concerns with Colin, Colin felt the same alarm and agreed that somehow the Seventh-day Adventist Church had been misrepresented. We also felt affronted that another church usurped Christ's authority to decide which churches constituted the body of Christ.

However, when the book *Questions on Doctrine* was published, neither Colin nor Russell initially identified it with that statement of Pastor Naden. Colin eagerly purchased a copy of the book, but as he read it through, he was disappointed. He felt that the book played down the role of the prophetic gift of Sister White. He also felt alarmed when he read in the book that the atonement was completed on the cross of Calvary. This he knew to be evangelical teaching, but certainly not Adventist truth. The statement that the atonement was completed on the cross, but the benefits of that atonement were now being applied in the heavenly sanctuary, did nothing to allay his fears.

Although he did not yet see the other great problem on the nature of Christ in the statements, he was concerned enough to approach the pastor of the Woollarha Church in Sydney, Pastor George Best, and assert, "I don't believe that book should have been printed." Pastor Best was surprised at Colin's comment but admitted that he had not read the book carefully at that time. However, other mature and experienced men were taking up the issue, none more courageously than Elder M. L. Andreasen. This Danish pastor was a retired Field Secretary of the General Conference, and had held other important positions in God's church, including New York and Minnesota Conference presidencies and the office of president of Union College. Some felt that he was upset because he had not been among the group chosen to dialogue with the two Evangelicals, but that was a totally unfounded conclusion. Elder Andreasen began to write letters to the churches to alert the membership to the crisis. There is no question that he stood faithful when champions were few. Among the warnings he gave was the following:

> We have reached a crisis in this denomination when leaders are attempting to enforce false doctrine and threaten those who object. The whole program is unbelievable. Men are now attempting to remove the foundation of many generations, and think they can succeed. If we did not have the Spirit of Prophecy, we would not know of the departure from sound doctrine which is now threatening us and the coming of the omega which will decimate our ranks and cause grievous wounds. The present situation has been clearly outlined. We are nearing the climax (*Letters to the Churches*, Number 3).

Another warrior to stand firm in his latter years was Dr. Benjamin G. Wilkinson. He is reported to have said that the book *Questions On Doctrine* is "a dagger aimed at the heart of the Seventh-day Adventist Church." (H. H. Meyers, *With Cloak and Dagger*, p. 5). However, those standing against this apostasy were few, and those who did stand were persecuted. In the end, the faithful warrior Andreasen lost his credentials and was considered an apostate. Indeed, it was determined that he would lose his sustentation, and had it not been for the Social Security Administration of the United States Government, he would have. However, the administration warned the General Conference that it would be acting illegally to deprive Elder Andreasen of his sustentation. After his death in 1962, his ministerial credentials were reinstated posthumously.

The answers given to Barnhouse and Martin as reported in *Questions On Doctrine* had undermined three of the most important beliefs of the Seventh-day Adventist Church:

1) The Atonement. It has been claimed that there is no biblical base for the final atonement taking place in the sanctuary. However, Seventh-day Adventists who have studied the sixteenth chapter of Leviticus will note that thirteen times the word "atonement" is used in that chapter, and the atonement was not completed until the blood was sprinkled on and before the mercy seat by the high priest (See Leviticus 16:15-17). In the anti-type, the atonement of Jesus could not be completed until He ministered His blood in the Most Holy Place of the heavenly sanctuary.

2) The Nature of Christ. As Dr. Ralph Larson has shown in his monumental work, *The Word Made Flesh*, all Seventh-day Adventist writers, including the prophetess herself, agreed from 1852-1952 that Christ took upon Himself our fallen nature. However, the book *Questions On Doctrine* strictly denies this consensus, claiming that He took man's unfallen nature. Such claims deny the very principles of righteousness by faith as proclaimed by Waggoner and Jones in and after 1888, and in the repeated statements of Sister White on this topic. Whereas consistently she talks of fallen and sinful nature in regard to Jesus' human nature, never once does she designate it as unfallen or sinless. Some have tried to use other statements of Sister White to raise questions against this truth, but their arguments cannot be sustained. Whenever Sister White is warning against making Jesus altogether like us, she is referring to either His character or His divine nature, certainly not His human nature.

3) The Role of Sister White. The role of Sister White is, to say the least, shaded in the book so that her prophetic role is clouded. This book was distributed by the hundreds of thousands and has played a major role in the tragic schism that now exists in the Seventh-day Adventist Church. As always, division has come through apostasy, not through truth. This book became the text-book for those embracing the New Theology, which was introduced in the 1970s and 1980s.

Thus, not only the doctrines mentioned above have been put aside, but virtually the whole foundation of our faith; the prophetic gift, the sanctuary message, the nature of man, the nature of salvation, the nature of sin, the gospel, and prophetic interpretation were step-by-step changed by many who claimed to be representing the authentic faith.

When men and women belatedly stood up to challenge this aberrant theology, they were considered to be divisive, critical, legalistic, and perfectionistic. Such false accusations discouraged many otherwise faithful people from becoming strongly involved in defending the faith delivered to the saints.

The statements of Dr. Barnhouse clearly confirmed these changes. Here is just one representation of his statements on these changes:

> It was perceived that the Adventists were strenuously denying certain doctrinal positions which had previously been attributed to them. For instance, they stated that "They repudiated absolutely the thought that seventh-day Sabbath-keeping was a basis for salvation. . ." (*Eternity,* September, 1956).

It is true that Sabbath-keeping is not a basis for salvation, nor does it invest us with merit in order to earn salvation. Such a view would constitute legalism; nevertheless, no one can be saved who understands this message and is not a true Sabbath-keeper.

As previously stated, the authors of *Questions On Doctrine* repudiated the time-honored belief in the fallen nature of Christ, denied the atoning work of Christ in the heavenly sanctuary, and greatly minimized the prophetic gift of Sister White. How such clearly anti-Adventist views could ever have been printed by our denomination is beyond understanding. Nevertheless, they have become the basis, not only for the New Theology, but also for the subsequent impotency in the church that has led to the Celebration movement, and now to the introduction of Neuro-Linguistic Programming and New Age concepts into the Seventh-day Adventist Church.

Because of the impotency of the New Theology, it has been thought necessary to use these worldly means to bring people back into the pews, when indeed the preaching of the gospel as delivered to the pioneers of this church would not only bring people back, but would also challenge them to ministry, and would bring many others into the Seventh-day Adventist Church, as it has done aforetime.

By the time that Elder Figuhr's successor, Elder Robert Pierson, became General Conference president in 1966, the devious seeds of apostasy had been well sown. During his presidency, Elder Pierson realized that dramatic changes were taking place, and thus in 1975 he put out his excellent book, *We Still Believe,* in an attempt to help the membership of the church understand the true pillars of our faith. When, in 1978, Elder Pierson retired, his message became very clear.

In his final address to the Annual Council, October 16, 1978, reported in the October 26 *Adventist Review,* he had this to say,

> Already, brethren and sisters, there are subtle forces that are beginning to stir. Regrettably there are those in the church who belittle the inspiration of the Bible, who scorn the first eleven chapters of Genesis, who question the Spirit of Prophecy's short chronology on the age of the earth, and who subtly and not-so-subtly attack the Spirit of Prophecy. There are some who point to the Reformers and contemporary theologians as a source and the norm of Seventh-day Adventist doctrine. There are those who allegedly are tired of the hackneyed phrases of Adventism. There are those who wish to forget the standards to the church we love. There are those who covet and would court the favor of the Evangelicals; who would throw off the mantle of a peculiar people; and those who would go the way of the secular, materialistic world. . . .

> Fellow leaders, beloved brothers and sisters—don't let it happen! I appeal to you as earnestly as I know how this morning—don't let it happen! I appeal to Andrews University, to

the seminary, to Loma Linda University—don't let it happen!
We are not Seventh-day Anglicans, not Seventh-day
Lutherans—we are Seventh-day Adventists! This is God's last
church with God's last message!. . .

In the fourth generation there is much machinery; the number
of administrators increases, while the number of workers at
the grass-roots level becomes proportionately less. Great church
councils are held to define doctrines. More schools, universi-
ties, and seminaries are established. These go to the world for
accreditation and tend to become secularized, there is a reex-
amination of positions and modernizing of methods. Attention is given to contemporary culture, with an interest in the
arts, music, architecture, literature. The movement seeks to
become "relevant" to contemporary society by becoming involved in popular causes. Services become formal. The group
enjoys complete acceptance by the world. The sect has become a church! . . .

And then I call attention to a vision the Lord's servant had, in
which she saw a ship heading towards an iceberg. She said,
"There, towering high above the ship, was a gigantic iceberg.
An authoritative voice cried out, `Meet it!' There was not a
moment's hesitation. It was time for instant action. The engi-
neer put on full steam, and the man at the wheel steered the
ship straight into the iceberg. With a crash he struck the ice.
There was a fearful shock, and the iceberg broke into many
pieces, falling with a noise like thunder to the deck. The
passengers were violently shaken by the force of the collision,
but no lives were lost. The vessel was injured, but not beyond
repair. She rebounded from the contact, trembling from stem
to stern, like a living creature. Then she moved forward on
her way." . . . Fellow leaders, it may be that in the not-too-
distant future you will have to meet it. I pray God will give
you grace and courage and wisdom (*Adventist Review,* October 26, 1978).

Elder Pierson, in two historic Annual Councils, along with
other leaders, including Elder Kenneth Wood, the editor of the
Review and Herald, tried to do everything to turn back the tide of
apostasy. In 1974 Elder Wood put out his monumental "Righteousness By Faith" issue of the *Review and Herald,* but nothing
seemed to be able to stand against the rising tide of apostasy and

the determination of those who were supporting it to change the beliefs and doctrines of the church and to turn the church toward ecumenism.

There is no question that Elder Pierson died a discouraged man, realizing just how determined those supporting apostasy in the church were to destroy the foundations of the faith. But just as God raised up Elder Pierson, He also continues to raise up others who will stand though the heavens fall, who are as true to principle as the needle is to the pole, men who cannot be bought or sold or bribed or threatened or flattered away from God's truth. Such men and women may still be in short supply, but God will use each one who will stand nobly in this time of test and trial.

7

The Organization of the Early Christian Church

The gospel of Mark presents the most direct record of the first Christian ordination service.

> And he goeth up into a mountain, and calleth unto him whom he would: and they came unto him. And he ordained twelve, that they should be with him, and that he might send them forth to preach, and to have power to heal sickness, and to cast out devils (Mark 3:13-15).

Thus, Jesus Himself ordained the first workers in the Christian church. He ordained them to be apostles with a two-fold mission: 1) to preach, and 2) to heal. Apart from Christ, the disciples were the first medical missionaries of the Christian church.

Matthew and Luke give further insights into the mission of the apostles.

> These twelve Jesus sent forth, and commanded them, saying, Go not into the way of the Gentiles, and into any city of the Samaritans enter ye not: But go rather to the lost sheep of the house of Israel. And as ye go, preach, saying, The kingdom of heaven is at hand. Heal the sick, cleanse the lepers, raise the dead, cast out devils: freely ye have received, freely give (Matthew 10:5-8).

> Then he called his twelve disciples together, and gave them power and authority over all devils, and to cure diseases. And he sent them to preach the kingdom of God, and to heal the sick. And he said unto them, Take nothing for your journey, neither staves, nor scrip, neither bread, neither money; neither have two coats apiece. And whatsoever house ye enter into, there abide, and thence depart. And whosoever will not receive you, when ye go out of that city, shake off the very dust from your feet for a testimony against them. And they departed, and went through the towns, preaching the gospel, and healing every where (Luke 9:1-6).

In sending the apostles to preach and to heal, Jesus gave them His very own ministry.

And Jesus went about all Galilee, teaching in their synagogues, and preaching the gospel of the kingdom, and healing all manner of sickness and all manner of disease among the people (Matthew 4:23).

Now after that John was put in prison, Jesus came into Galilee, preaching the gospel of the kingdom of God, and saying, The time is fulfilled, and the kingdom of God is at hand: repent ye, and believe the gospel (Mark 1:14,15).

Though the apostles were still immature in their understanding and in their training, Jesus sent them out to experience the power of preaching and to share the great gospel. We will note that He ordained them to preach the gospel of the kingdom. They could not at this time have had a full understanding of the gospel because of their own inadequate understanding even of the mission and ministry of Christ. Nevertheless, they could declare Jesus as the promised Messiah, the one who would establish His kingdom. Not until later did they understand the fullness of this message. The words of Christ to them just before His crucifixion, recorded in the great second advent chapter of Matthew, must have been imbedded in their minds until their deaths.

And this gospel of the kingdom shall be preached in all the world for a witness unto all nations; and then shall the end come (Matthew 24:14).

Of all the apostles, no doubt, John was privileged more than any other to understand the nature of this gospel.

And I saw another angel fly in the midst of heaven, having the everlasting gospel to preach unto them that dwell on the earth, and to every nation, and kindred, and tongue, and people, saying with a loud voice, Fear God, and give glory to him; for the hour of his judgement is come: and worship him that made heaven, and earth, and the sea, and the fountains of waters (Revelation 14:6,7).

After the resurrection of Jesus the disciples had the assurance that this gospel would go to every human being on the face of the planet. They also had the privilege in the time of John to understand the full message of the gospel.* This gospel became the all-consuming passion of the apostles after Jesus' ascension to heaven.

---

* See *Adventism Proclaimed*, R. R. Standish and C. D. Standish, Hartland Publications, P.O. Box 1, Rapidan, VA 22733, USA.

When they had received the mighty power of the Holy Ghost in their upper room experience, they went out to share this gospel with men and women of their day, first in Jerusalem, then Judea, then Samaria, and then to the uttermost parts of the earth. In fact, the Spirit so impelled them that nothing could prevent them from presenting this gospel to the world. When the rulers and elders commanded them not to teach in the name of Jesus, Peter and John responded in a manner that is the pattern for every true, dedicated, and converted Christian.

> But Peter and John answered and said unto them, Whether it be right in the sight God to hearken unto you more than unto God, judge ye. For we cannot but speak the things which we have seen and heard (Acts 4:19,20).

Later, when challenged again, they answered with these powerful words,

> Then Peter and the other apostles answered and said, we ought to obey God rather than men (Acts 5:29).

With such conviction, the gospel went all over the world. Paul could declare concerning the gospel, that it

> was preached to every creature which is under heaven. (Colossians 1:23).

God's ministry today has this same challenge.

However, very quickly other considerations took the apostles' attention away from the work Christ had ordained them to do. They had been given only two commissions, to preach the gospel and to heal the sick, but conflict arose in the church. There were widows, orphans, and the needy—all who needed care and attention. And the apostles became so embroiled in these needs that the work for which Christ had ordained them was greatly hindered. Furthermore, they became involved in jealous disputes. At this point they had to change their direction and return to the responsibility of evangelism, so they instructed the brethren to appoint others to fill the church's physical needs.

> Then the twelve called the multitude of the disciples unto them, and said, It is not reason that we should leave the word of God, and serve tables. Wherefore, brethren, look ye out

among you seven men of honest report, full of the Holy Ghost and wisdom, whom we may appoint over this business. But we will give ourselves continually to prayer, and to the ministry of the word (Acts 6:2-4).

From this decision the disciples chose six godly men to care for the physical needs of the people. These were ordained to be deacons in the church. Paul defined well the qualifications of a deacon.

Men of honest report, full of the Holy Ghost and wisdom (Acts 6:3).

Likewise must the deacons be grave, not doubletongued, not given to much wine, not greedy of filthy lucre; Holding the mystery of the faith in a pure conscience. And let these also first be proved; then let them use the office of a deacon, being found blameless. Even so must their wives be grave, not slanderers, sober, faithful in all things. Let the deacons be the husbands of one wife, ruling their children and their own houses well. For they that have used the office of a deacon well purchase to themselves a good degree, and great boldness in the faith which is in Christ Jesus (1 Timothy 3:8-13).

How important that the church bestow this high office of deacon only upon the most godly and righteous men within the church. It is the role of the deacons to care for the needs of the poor, the afflicted, the aged, the widows, and the orphans. The deacons have the responsibility to bring to the lives of each member that which will sustain them and uphold them.

The scriptures refer to another group of ordained men called the elders. This is not a new term, for elders were chosen in Old Testament times. But now elders were to fulfill a new role.

The first record of the ordination of elders comes during the ministry of Paul and Barnabas in the cities of Asia Minor: Lystra, Iconium, and Antioch.

And when they had ordained them elders in every church, and had prayed with fasting, they commended them to the Lord, on whom they believed (Acts 14:23).

On Paul and Barnabas's return to Jerusalem, the elders were certainly well in place, for we read,

And when they were come to Jerusalem, they were received of
the church, and of the apostles and elders, and they declared
all things that God had done with them (Acts 15:4).

Unlike the appointment of the first deacons, the New Testament indicates no clear point when elders were chosen in the
church. This may be because the role of an elder predated Christianity. We know the elders held high responsibility in the early
Christian church because, when some of the brethren claimed that
all males had to be circumcised according to the Law of Moses,
we learn,

And the apostles and elders came together for to consider of
this matter (Acts 15:6).

At this Jerusalem Council the issue of Judaism became the
central theme.

What was the role of these elders? In writing to Titus, Paul
indicated their senior responsibility in each city,

And ordain elders in every city, as I had appointed thee
(Titus 1:5).

These elders had oversight of the churches and were the spiritual leaders of the local church community. Peter exhorts them,
however, in the way they were to lead in the church.

The elders which are among you I exhort, who am also an
elder, and a witness of the sufferings of Christ, and also a
partaker of the glory that shall be revealed: Feed the flock of
God which is among you, taking the oversight thereof, not by
constraint, but willingly; nor for filthy lucre, but of a ready
mind; neither as being lords over God's heritage, but being
ensamples to the flock (1 Peter 5:1-3).

In the early church these elders were also called bishops. Paul
gives a number of qualifications for a bishop. For example, if
someone desired to be a bishop, Paul had this counsel,

If a man desire the office of a bishop, he desireth a good
work. A bishop then must be blameless, the husband of one
wife, vigilant, sober, of good behaviour, given to hospitality,
apt to teach; Not given to wine, no striker, not greedy of filthy
lucre; but patient, not a brawler, not covetous; One that ruleth
well his own house, having his children in subjection with all

gravity; (for if a man know not how to rule his own house, how shall he take care of the church of God?) not a novice, lest being lifted up with pride he fall into the condemnation for the devil. Moreover he must have a good report of them which are without; lest he fall into reproach and the snare of the devil (1 Timothy 3:1-7).

Paul gives some further qualifications in his epistle to Titus.

For a bishop must be blameless, as a steward of God; not selfwilled, not soon angry, not given to wine, no striker, not given to filthy lucre; but a lover of hospitality, a lover of good men, sober, just, holy, temperate; holding fast the faithful word as he hath been taught, that he may be able by sound doctrine both to exhort and to convince the gainsayers (Titus 1:7-9).

Paul also understood that in certain circumstances it would be appropriate to financially support these elders.

Let the elders that rule well be counted worthy of double honour, especially they who labour in the word and doctrine. For the scripture saith, Thou shalt not muzzle the ox that treadeth out the corn. And, The labourer is worthy of his reward (1 Timothy 5:17,18).

The role of an elder was an extraordinarily important one. It included: 1) the leadership of the church, 2) the teaching of doctrine to the church members, 3) the anointing of the sick (see James 5:14).

The three basic roles of the church leaders in early apostolic times were 1) The apostles, being the evangelists, who were placed in the vanguard of soul winning, 2) the deacons who cared for the physical and emotional needs of the congregation, and 3) the elders who were responsible leaders of the local church community.

The women in the early Christian church also fulfilled specific roles. We know of the ministry of Lydia, a seller of purple from the city of Thyatira. (Acts 16:14,15). Also, we see the wonderful testimony concerning Dorcas of Joppa, a woman "full of good works and almsdeeds." (Acts 9:36) She became the role model for every deaconess.

The early Christian church developed the major roles needed to care for the mental, spiritual, and physical needs of the members of God's church and for the church's evangelistic thrusts. This is the paradigm for God's church today. God ordained this organization to fulfill the mission and ministry of His end-time church.

8

Divine Form of Church Governance

When the Seventh-day Adventist Church began its mission of destiny, the members coming from various churches in the United States naturally had different views on the structure and governance of the emerging church. They considered basically three forms of church governance. The first was the hierarchical form of church governance. This was also know as the papal form, for all Protestant churches had rejected this form of church organization.

The hierarchical form of church governance is built upon an individual or a small committee, who is/are responsible for making the major, momentous decisions of the church. The Roman Catholic Church is the archetype of hierarchal church governance. At the head of this church its leader, the pope, when speaking ex cathedra, has absolute authority. Whether by a papal bull or by a papal encyclical, the pope's directives are expected to be accepted without modifications, additions, or deletions. Enforcing this expectation has not always been easy for the Roman Catholic Church. This was especially true during the nineteenth century, when the papal influence reached an unprecedented low. To help strengthen papal authority, the longest-reigning pope in history, Pius IX, put forward the doctrine of papal infallibility. That doctrine was meant to add the weight of divine authority to the pontifical pronouncements. This doctrine of infallibility was not accepted without considerable opposition, but its proponents eventually prevailed.

In the hierarchal system the leader makes the decisions. These directives are expected to pass down through the archdiocese (archbishopric) to the diocese (bishopric) to the local parish congregations without modification or change of any kind. The dictates of the leader are binding upon all members of the church. We live in an age where not a few are challenging such absolute authority; nevertheless, most Roman Catholics around the world accept the edicts of the pope as final and non-negotiable.

The episcopal form of governance was also known at the time of the commencement of the Seventh-day Adventist Church. The Anglican Church in England developed this form, and the Episcopal Church of America carried it on after the Declaration of American Independence. Such a system has no supreme pontiff. The authority resides at the level of the bishop.

In England, for example, there are well over 500 such bishops, but only two archbishops, the Archbishop of Canterbury and the Archbishop of York. The Archbishop of Canterbury is called the primate of Great Britain, and while the reigning monarch is the leader of the Anglican Church, decision-making authority is vested at the level of the diocese in the hands of the bishops. The episcopal form of church governance has some of the elements of the hierarchal system, but is less centralized. Each bishop is almost a law unto himself in terms of his authority. Naturally, some bishops exercise more autocratic authority than do others, but the running of the dioceses are largely in their hands.

In recent years, the Anglican Church has felt a deep frustration with this form of governance. Indeed, the former Archbishop of Canterbury, Dr. Robert Runcie, urged the Anglican Church to reunite with the Church of Rome under a reformed Papacy. In a sense, the Anglican Church structure is readily adaptable to this reunion for it already possesses a modified hierarchal structure.

The third form of church governance known to the pioneers of the Seventh-day Adventist Church was the congregational form. Here every church had its own autonomy. One can see this kind of governance best in the Congregational Church, the Baptist Church, the Church of Christ, and similar churches. While a loose organization exists amongst these churches, nevertheless, each church has its own autonomy. For example, the church congregation has the right to hire or fire its own pastor. The church handles its own finances and accepts special missionary projects. It is not uncommon for a church to sponsor a missionary family overseas and guarantee its financial needs.

The hierarchal and episcopal forms of church governance were wholly unacceptable to the early believers of the Seventh-day Adventist Church. They naturally had an inclination toward the congregational form of church governance. These pioneers were usually very independent people who had been persecuted by the various churches from which they came. They wanted as much freedom as possible to exercise their religious convictions. However, God did not choose the congregational form of church governance, but rather the representative form of church governance for His remnant people.

In this form of church governance, the emerging structure of the Seventh-day Adventist Church had most of its authority placed in the hands of the local churches. The churches had the responsibility to accept new members. Once they became the members of the local church community they were members of the church at large, or what later became the worldwide Seventh-day Adventist Church. The local churches alone had the responsibility to discipline unfaithful members. The local church was specifically responsible for the missionary endeavors within the region of its locality, whether it be a rural region or a town or city. Indeed, the whole authority of the church has its base in the local church community, as will be seen in subsequent chapters of this book.

As other areas of organization developed, first the local conferences, then the General Conference, much later the unions, and finally the divisions of the General Conference, each one was delegated responsibility. Every level was designated to serve the needs of the level whose representatives had elected its leaders. But ultimately all the levels received their authority from the local churches and served the needs and interests of these rapidly expanding local church communities. The conferences were not only established to serve the needs of the local churches but also, more importantly, to plan and organize the expansion of the work into areas, towns, and cities where there was no Seventh-day Adventist presence. Thus developed the representative form of church governance that God had ordained for the Seventh-day Adventist Church.

In so ordaining, God gave a form of governance that allowed for checks and balances, and which was meant to decentralize the levels of authority. While today we still have the vestiges of the representative form of church governance, in reality we have shifted alarmingly toward the hierarchal form. In so doing, we wittingly or unwittingly rebel against God.

9

The Development of Structure in the Seventh-day Adventist Church

After the Great Disappointment of 1844, individuals, families, and in some cases small groups of Adventists were scattered around the United States, especially in the New England area and upstate New York. However, these Adventists fragmented from each other very quickly. They divided into Sabbathkeeping and Sunday-keeping groups. Later, the issue of the Spirit of Prophecy caused other schisms to take place. Those who did remain true to the revelations of the Advent Message became fervent in missionary work. However, so few and so scattered were these early Adventist groups that they are often referred to by Sister White as the "little flock" or the "scattered flock." As more joined the ranks of God's remnant church, little church buildings began to materialize—some of them not larger than sufficient to contain a congregation of thirty to sixty. Usually, they were little weatherboard churches, but the Holy Spirit was unquestionably manifest in a mighty way in those churches. Each of those churches became a light to spread the truth in its immediate region.

It soon became obvious, however, that though this helped, there needed to be an organized structure that could plan more directly to expand the message of salvation into regions where no Seventh-day Adventist presence existed. Thus, in 1861, the first state conference was established, the Michigan Conference. It is of no little interest that a chairman rather than a president was chosen for the Michigan Conference. Joseph Bates was the chosen chairman of the conference. This was in line with the desire to avoid any semblance of a papal form of governance. The people did not want a "king" to rule over them. They considered that concept to be wholly out of harmony with the governance that God had ordained.

Now the work of God could be planned better in order to send workers into unentered towns, cities, and counties. In this way, God's workers hoped to establish new church communities all around the conferences. This plan worked very effectively, and soon they organized quite a number of other conferences, among them Ohio, Iowa, and Kansas. This broader base of organization made it possible for the work of God to expand quite quickly.

However, even that did not provide planning for states where an Adventist presence had not already been established. Conferences had been established only in states where a number of strong, viable churches already existed. As the population of the United States rapidly moved westward into the frontier territories, God's people saw that such conferences obviously did nothing to accommodate the new emerging populations in the West. They needed an organization to foster the message in unentered regions. The issue of the Civil War also proved a factor. During this war, government authorities gave Adventist young men a very difficult time because of their determination not to participate. Thus, they realized a need to establish a General Conference which would plan the work with a broad base and be able to foster the development of new missionary effort in other parts of the United States. A General Conference would also give our young men a legal basis for their conscientious stand against participation in war. A third factor influencing the need for a General Conference was the need for a legal body to hold title to certain church properties such as the conference offices and the publishing houses.

Notwithstanding the fact that God had confirmed the need for the organization of the General Conference, fierce opposition to its development arose. Some claimed that James White was seeking power. Because of this opposition, James White refused to become the first president of the General Conference, and that honor was accorded to John Byington, a less-known, older leader of the emerging Seventh-day Adventist Church.

It will be recalled that the establishment of the General Conference took place long before the sending out of the first missionary beyond the shores of North America. Indeed, it was formed before there was an Adventist presence of any significance in most of the United States.

As the mission efforts of the 1870s and 1880s brought a worldwide presence to the Seventh-day Adventist Church, it was clear that even the organizations of local churches, local conferences, and the General Conference did not give adequate opportunity for expansion and development of the Seventh-day Adventist

Church. At one stage in the 1880s, loose districts were established in the United States which covered large regions of the country. When, in 1895, the Australasian Union was formed, it set a precedent which became the archetype of the unions that were established at the 1901 General Conference in Battle Creek, Michigan. The unions were to direct the work in broader territories than the conferences.

As the work of God expanded worldwide, even the unions did not adequately bridge the gap between the leadership in the General Conference and the work in the more localized areas. The first region to be called a division was the European Division, and this became the archetype of the 1918 formation of the divisions of the General Conference. The divisions do not operate in the same way as a union, a local conference, or a local church operates. They are indeed divisions of the General Conference. Thus, it is not the North American Division of the General Conference, but the General Conference of Seventh-day Adventists, North American Division; it is not the Trans-European Division, but the General Conference of Seventh-day Adventists, Trans-European Division, and so on. These divisions are regional offices of the General Conference. Thus, the president of each division is also a vice-president of the General Conference. Because the divisions are part of the General Conference level, they do not send delegates per se to the General Conference Session; rather, delegates are sent by the unions. This is the reason that the officers and departmental leaders of each division are elected at each General Conference session.

As we review chart one (page 74), it is evident that God ordained an inverted pyramidal organization. This is the basis of a representative form of church governance. The major responsibility is at the level of the local church. The purpose for the establishment of the conferences was not to exercise dominion over the local churches, but rather to serve them and more directly to plan for and provide for the expansion and development of the work in a particular state or territory. So, too, the union was established to provide an even broader base of development, so that the work could be developed more evenly. The General Conference has the responsibility of forwarding the work encompassing a worldwide vision.

This is not to say that each level of the church organization does not have authority, but that such authority is primarily that which is vested at each level by the representatives of the previous level. For example, the authority of the local conference is only that which is vested in it by the constituent churches of that conference. Thus, at a constituency meeting, representatives of the local churches have the authority to increase or decrease the responsibility of the local conference, to modify it or expand it.

It is the constituents' responsibility to decide who should constitute the nominating committee. This responsibility includes deciding what proportion of laity and ministry will be in the committee. Furthermore, the authority to decide what kind of officers and departmental directors they desire rests with the constituent local churches. For example, it is wholly within the hands of these delegates to decide whether to vote to have a secretary and a treasurer, or to combine the roles in one individual. They hold responsibility for deciding how many departmental men will serve, and in what capacities. It is even within their authority to divide the conference into two conferences, or to unite with another conference. They also must decide who are the members of the Conference Executive Committee for the ensuing term.

Thus, the choice of delegates for conference sessions should be very carefully considered after sincere prayer. Only men and women who have shown, by test and trial, that they love God and have a love for truth and righteousness should be considered for such an important responsibility. Men and women who are not afraid to speak up, and who have the courage of their convictions, are the only ones who should be considered for such a duty. It is not good enough to say, "Well, who is going to be available for the constituency meeting?" The choice must be made in a timely fashion, so that the most responsible representatives have time to plan to be there. The delegates should be asked to stay throughout the constituency meeting, no matter how long it might last. Too often, laity do not understand the grave responsibilities that God has placed before them, and therefore they take the responsibility lightly, or feel it is their duty simply to confirm the suggestions of the conference leadership. In fact, the laity have the responsibility of placing the most urgent issues before the constituency meeting.

All too often, resolutions voted for at the General Conference level are voted for at constituency meetings as if they are routine measures, and little dialogue or prayer is entered into. The approach that such a resolution must be accepted because it was voted for at the General Conference level, surely is a shade of papal mentality. Even though the resolution may have great merit, it may need modification at the local level in different regions of the world, or for different cultures. The laity may note a danger not perceived by denominational leaders. A typical example is the Perth Declaration voted in at the 1991 Annual Council. While having some heartwarming affirmations, it nevertheless had some deep forebodings for faithful lay ministries. It set the stage for denominational discipline of many who expose the rampaging apostasy and worldliness in the church. Many lay delegates at the constituency meetings recognized the danger, but few challenged the Perth Declaration—a decision they are sure to regret in the future.

It is our considered observation that most of the apostasy that has flooded into the Seventh-day Adventist Church, has been introduced by pastors and teachers. However, the laity share responsibility when they do not actively stand against the apostasy. They have the massive voting power to reject all of Satan's attempts to introduce error into our midst. With major doctrinal apostasy and issues such as Celebration, Neuro-Linguistic Programming, clown "ministry", drama, competitive sports, puppetry, and many other forms of irreverent activities invading the church, there is a decided need for active lay involvement in the destiny of God's church. Had there been an alert and responsible laity, the "New Theology" would have been cut short at its commencement, as would have been the Celebration movement. The inroads of humanism and deception as taught in Lab One and Lab Two (of Neuro-Linguistic Programming) would not have been tolerated, and not even the first thread of competitive sports would have been allowed to persist in our schools. The only way that true repentance—resulting in reformation and revival in the church— can take place is wide-ranging support from the laity and a determined effort, irrespective of the cost, to stand as true to principle as the proverbial needle to the pole.

God has placed at the local church level the responsibility to decide who will be accepted into the Seventh-day Adventist Church as new members. This, too, is an extremely important task. Too often, the acceptance of either new members or transfer members is a perfunctory act, and most of those voting have little or no idea of the new member's loyalty to God, His truth, and His principles. It is incumbent that the members of each church take this very critical role seriously. Once a member is voted into a local church, he or she becomes a member of the world-wide Seventh-day Adventist Church. Not only God, but also Satan, is bringing members into the church. Recognizing this, it is our responsibility to do everything we can within the parameters of human judgment, guided by the Holy Spirit, to accept only those who give evidence of being true Seventh-day Adventists.

God has also placed the authority in the hands of the local church, in the matter of disciplining members. Neither a conference, a union, or even the General Conference can dismiss a member of a local church; all they can do is recommend such. Conferences have sometimes obtained their goals by threats and promised recriminations. However, the laity still have the numbers to resist such un-Christ-like pressure. The local church membership alone has the authority to decide to disfellowship a member. This cannot be done by the pastor or the board, though both may make recommendations. Sadly, when put under pressure some members yield, and others decide not to attend meetings which have been called to make decisions about discipline, as if this would absolve them from the responsibility that God has placed in their hands.

Of course, there are valid reasons for disfellowshipment. When there is a serious deviation from truth or righteousness, a member should be separated from the body of the church. However, often those who are standing faithful to God, His truth, and His church are the ones being disfellowshiped by those who have abandoned the faith once delivered to the saints. Of course, the step of disfellowshiping should not be taken without great efforts to restore the one who has fallen, to bring him back into the fold of God's church. Disfellowshipment must never be based upon the failure of members to meet unscriptural and improper demands. Nevertheless, we cannot leave unfaithful men and women as members of the church. Today, with only about two in five members being in church on any given Sabbath in North America, and at least a third to a half being absent worldwide, large numbers of unfaithful Seventh-day Adventists obviously still remain on the membership rolls of local churches. Such a state brings great impotency to the church. We need to ask ourselves the question, What would happen if a large number of these unfaithful members turned up at a church business meeting? Allowing this present state within the church to continue is wrong.

Another responsibility God placed at the local church level is the adding of new churches and the disbanding of apostate churches. This can be done at a duly called constituency meeting of the sisterhood of churches of a local conference. A conference committee can recommend, but it cannot add a church to the sisterhood. Thereiore, it is incumbent upon the representatives of each church to investigate closely the development and the direction of any company that is applying to become a member of the sisterhood of churches. Likewise, it is outside the power of the conference committee to disband a church. Only two groups have this prerogative: the members of the church itself in question, and the delegates of the constituent churches. If the second group decides to take this measure, there must first be a peer group review in which the representatives of the church in question have the right to explain any possible questions concerning their beliefs or practices.

God designed that the conference is to serve the local church, not that the local church serve the conference. In like manner, the union serves the needs of the constituent conferences, and the General Conference the needs of the unions. That does not mean that the local conference, the union, and the General Conference do not have authority. All have authority, but it is that authority which has been vested in them by the constituents that have established them. Thus Sister White could say in 1909,

God has ordained that the representatives of His church from all parts of the earth, when assembled in a General Conference, shall have authority (*Testimonies for the Church*, Volume 9, p. 261).

Notice that it is not the General Conference Committee, but the representatives from all around the world (from the constituent unions) that have authority under the authority of God. However, this does not mean that the decisions of such delegates are infallible. Only God and His Word are infallible.

A typical example of the fallibility of even a General Conference in session occurred at the 1895 General Conference Session. At that time, Elder S. N. Haskell was in Africa. Cecil Rhodes, then premier of the Cape Colony, had granted him a large tract of land for the establishment of a school in what later became known as Rhodesia, and is now called Zimbabwe. The General Conference in session voted against acceptance of the property, and asked Elder Haskell to return it. Haskell was devastated and wrote to Sister White in Australia. He pointed out that this was not a government grant, for at the time Rhodesia was operated independently of the British government by the British East Africa Company. Sister White agreed with Haskell, and strongly condemned the action taken at the General Conference Session. That is but one example where the prophetess strongly disagreed with the action of the General Conference in session.

We cannot overlook her bitter sorrow when the General Conference in session turned away from the Lord's counsel at the 1901 and 1903 General Conference Sessions. Though the General Conference in session does have strong God-given authority, that authority falls short of infallibility; otherwise, we would be placing ourselves in a position similar to the papal authority of the Roman Catholic Church. That would be anathema to Adventism, because it is anathema to God.

God's Church Organization

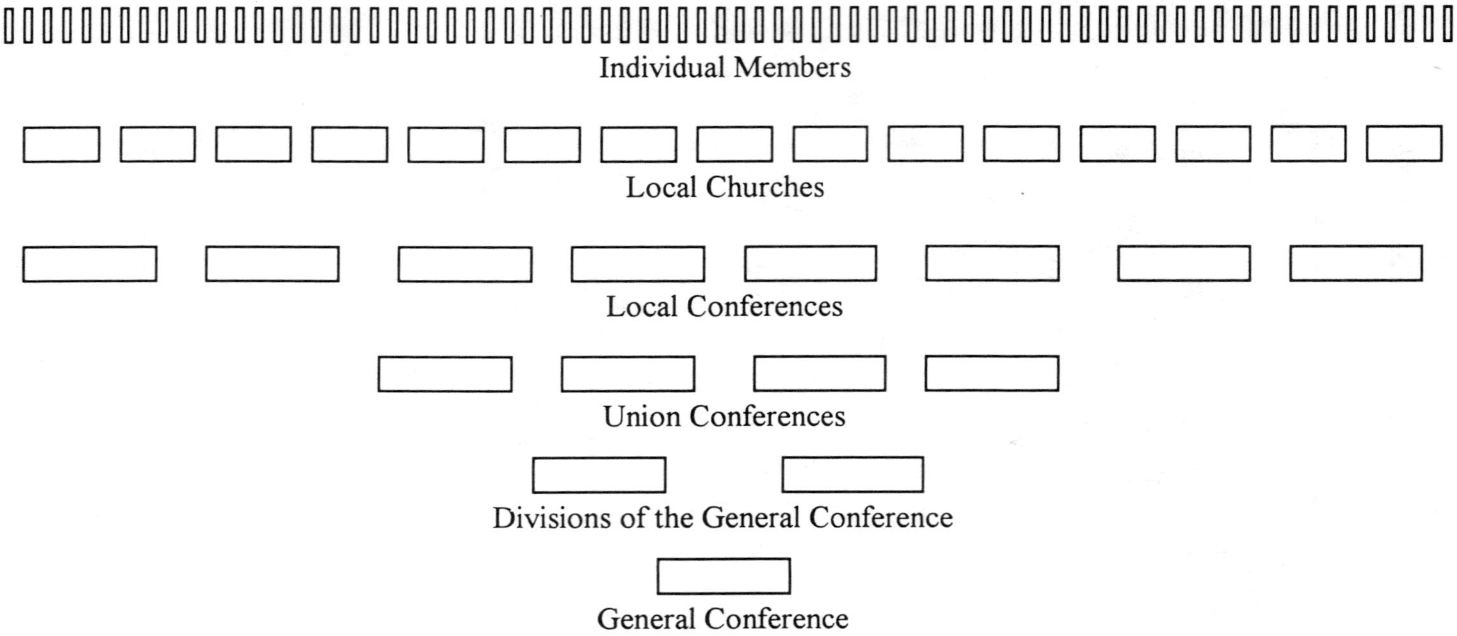

Individual Members

Local Churches

Local Conferences

Union Conferences

Divisions of the General Conference

General Conference

Chart 1

10

When There Were No
Church Pastors

I n the early years of the Seventh-day Adventist Church, God's people made no plans for church pastors as we know them today. As the infant church developed, the ministers itinerated between the little companies of believers, bringing inspiration and understanding to the precious souls. However, as churches began to multiply, and the congregations began to increase, a desire naturally arose to have full-time gospel workers associated with these churches. The pattern in the fallen churches of Protestantism was very clear. Each major church congregation had its own pastor, and if it was large enough, several pastors. Each small church shared a pastor with one or more other churches, but each had a pastor.

As would be expected, some of those in the new Adventist Church looked to pattern the work of the Seventh-day Adventist ministry after the churches from which they had come. But Sister White insisted that the role of the minister, as in apostolic times, was to move into new territories in order to enter into front-line evangelism where the message was non-existent or particularly weak.

> When the ministers understand the great blessing to be derived from laboring for those who know not the truth, they will leave the churches, after impressing upon them the importance of devising plans and methods whereby they can do within their borders the same kind of work that the ministers of the gospel are doing in the regions beyond (*Medical Ministry*, p. 318).

> Instead of keeping the ministers at work for the churches that already know the truth, let the members of the churches say to these laborers: "Go work for souls that are perishing in darkness. We ourselves will carry forward the services of the church. We will keep up the meetings, and, by abiding in Christ, will maintain spiritual life. We will work for souls that are about us, and we will send our prayers and our gifts to sustain the laborers in more needy and destitute fields" (*Testimonies for the Church*, vol. 6, p. 30).

As a general rule, the conference laborers should go out from the churches into new fields, using their God-given ability to a purpose in seeking and saving the lost (*Evangelism,* p. 382).

If the ministers would get out of the way, if they would go forth into new fields, the members would be obliged to bear responsibilities, and their capabilities would increase by use (Ibid.).

Thus, the early Seventh-day Adventist church began to develop district pastors. These were not district pastors as we understand them today—pastors in charge of two or more churches—but rather pastors who were each appointed to an area in which to conduct evangelistic meetings. It became common for the conferences to divide their territories up into districts and to appoint a pastor to proclaim the Word in each district.

We had the privilege to grow up, until the age of about fourteen, while this system was still employed in the work of God in Australia. (This system apparently changed earlier in the United States than in Australia.) We were also privileged to have for our father the "young" elder of the Hamilton Church in the city of Newcastle, Australia. This permitted us as lads to gain an understanding of the function of the pastor and of the officers of the church in such an organizational pattern.

A pastor would be appointed to a district. If it was in a city, it would be a city district. Our city of Newcastle at that time had a population of about a quarter of a million people, and so was considered one district. In the more rural areas, a pastor would be appointed to a district which might contain three or four sizeable towns. The major function of the pastor was that of proclaiming the Word of God to those not of our faith. The pastor would locate within the district. If assigned to a rural district, he would conduct a five- to six-months crusade in one town, usually holding meetings two nights a week and spending the rest of the time in visitation, presentation of Bible studies, and other soul-winning activities. He would then likely hold a crusade in a different town in his rural district each succeeding year until being transferred to another district. The evangelist appointed to a city district might also hold a crusade for five or six months of each year, but in varying suburbs instead of towns. After three or four years, the pastor in either type of district was usually transferred to another district.

It was usual for the pastor and his family to become members of one of the churches within the district. The first part of the year was given over to organizing the church or churches within the area to provide support for the crusade in the various functions necessary. The church members always received great encouragement through involving themselves in the crusade by their presence at each meeting, by their financial support, and by doing the various jobs so often associated with crusades—folding leaflets and distributing them house-to-house, etc. Some were always chosen to help with such tasks as ushering, presenting music, and singing in the choir, which were so much a feature of those evangelist efforts.

Because of this method, we had the privilege of attending crusades every year during our youth. Our parents were the kind of parents who took their boys with them to attend not only the first meeting or two, but also almost every other meeting in the crusade. What a great privilege it was for us to hear every year the great truths of the Advent faith couched within the prophetic utterances of Scripture! We have no question that the privilege has been a wonderful bastion of truth in our own understanding of God's Word and the destiny of the Adventist movement.

It is important to recognize that conferences did not always have sufficient funds for all the pastors in the various districts to run crusades, but that this did not alter the basic function of the minister. Each minister was required to put soul-winning first, and if the conference did not have the budget to run a public evangelistic campaign, the minister would be responsible for personal work. He often did door-to-door work, sometimes using the literature ministry as an approach to souls interested in the third angel's message. Whether by public evangelism or by personal evangelism, the pastor's primary role was like that of the apostles of the New Testament: bringing the gospel of Jesus Christ to those who at that time knew it not.

Let us examine what took place in the local churches in that era. We can speak from the experience that we had in the Hamilton Church in Newcastle. The pastor appointed to our district would preach once a month in our church. That is not to say that he would not preach in other churches during that month, and normally he did. However, it was most extraordinary for the pastor to attend a business meeting or a board meeting, and certainly he took no part in a nominating committee. This was true even if he and his family had become members of our church. The pastor kept too busy in soul-winning endeavors and in Bible studies to spend time in an activity that the laity of the church could wholly and more effectively handle themselves. This practice was in harmony with Sister White's counsel.

Not a few ministers are neglecting the very work that they have been appointed to do. Why are those who are set apart for the work of the ministry placed on committees and boards? Why are they called upon to attend so many business meetings, many times at great distance from their fields of labor? Why are not business matters placed in the hands of businessmen? The ministers have not been set apart to do this work. The finances of the cause are to be properly managed by men of ability, but ministers are set apart for another line of work. Let the management of financial matters rest on others than those ordained to the ministry.

> Ministers are not to be called hither and thither to attend board meetings for the purpose of deciding common business questions. Many of our ministers have done this work in the past, but it is not the work in which the Lord wishes them to engage. Too many financial burdens have been placed on them. When they try to carry these burdens, they neglect to fulfill the gospel commission. God looks upon this as a dishonor to His name (*Testimonies for the Church*, vol. 7, pp. 254, 255).

> The world is to be warned. Ministers should work earnestly and devotedly, opening new fields and engaging in personal labor for souls, instead of hovering over the churches that already have great light and many advantages (Ibid., pp. 255).

Furthermore, in God's plan for lay ministry, there were no senior elders, senior deacons, or senior deaconesses. Elders, deacons, and deaconesses were chosen, but there was no discrimination of rank. As the time for a board or business meeting approached, in a wholly informal way, one of the elders would say, "Now who chaired the last meeting?" Usually they would eventually remember, and then they would decide whose turn it was. Each took his turn in leadership. They were following the admonition of Jesus, "All ye are brethren," (Matthew 23:8). Thus, no one had kingly rule in the church, and the teams worked together in excellent harmony.

When we were nine, our family shifted to live with our grandfather after the death of our grandmother. As the house had only two bedrooms, we slept in what had formerly been the dining room, straight off the kitchen. Here we could easily overhear the conversations between our father and mother concerning the activities of the church. Often when our father came home after a business or board meeting, our mother naturally asked, "Was anything important decided tonight?" It became very obvious to us from the dialogues of our parents that there was a great deal of unity and tranquility within the church. There seemed to be few times when any major issues arose to cause division among those who were on the board. Our church had a harmony which many churches today crave.

The lay leadership of the church held responsibility for almost every aspect of what took place. Commonly, the elders, deacons, and deaconesses, in a somewhat informal way, met after the divine service on Sabbath in order to dialogue concerning any member(s) who had missed the church service. Thus, often someone would ask the question, "Did anyone see Brother or Sister X here today?" If none had seen that person, the church board members would decide who would go to visit the family that afternoon. We well remember, a number of times, bicycling with our parents to shut-ins to bring spiritual strength to them and encourage them during their illnesses. Hospital visits were organized in much the same way. Thus the laity were given the responsibility of spiritually blessing those who could not attend church.

If any member appeared lax or backslidden in their Christian experience, the elders would shoulder the responsibility of seeking to restore such a member. In this way the lay leadership was responsible for the physical and spiritual needs of the members of the church. They handled the usual domestic problems that arose or the challenges that families had because of poverty or other adversity. The district pastors had little or no responsibility in these areas, as the primary focus of their ministry was to work for those not of our faith.

When the time approached for the quarterly communion service, the elders, deacons, and deaconesses frequently met together and formed themselves into teams of three. Each team of one elder, deacon, and deaconess would visit shut-ins and administer the communion to them. Thus the total functioning of the local church was where God wanted it to be, in the hands of the laity. Not until the end of the 1940s was the first church pastor per se appointed to our church.

Recently, we spoke with Pastor O. K. Anderson, at the time eighty-six years of age, who had gone through this whole experience. We simply asked, "Why did we change from district pastors to church pastors?"

His answer was simple, "Because the ministers felt it was too hard to be constantly evangelizing; they felt it would be easier to pastor the local church." Others have sensed that the tragic change in local church governance was due to a desire for our churches to operate according to the failed pattern of the fallen churches of the world. In any case, the change did occur.

After the appointment of our first church pastor, we noticed as youth that our father returned home from board and business meetings somewhat confused. He did not know how to handle one who, in reality, immediately became a "king" in the church. The pastor assumed a place that indicated he was above the rest in the meetings. Our father did not always agree with the recommendation or the stance taken by the pastor, yet he wanted to show respect and loyalty, and thus he was not sure how he could disagree respectfully with the pastor. It was indeed a difficult time for our father and, no doubt, for other lay leaders in the church as well. Now the pastor had the leadership of the church. No longer were those who exercised leadership in the church equal brethren.

Today we have seen great changes because of this alteration of governance at the local church level. It has led to our pastors fulfilling most of the roles of the elders and deacons and few of the roles for which they were ordained. It is common now for laity to say, "Pastor, Mrs. Smith is sick, please visit her," or "Mr. Jones is in the hospital, can you get over to see him?" This alteration has encouraged ineffectiveness and laziness in the laity, and has imperiled their spiritual destiny. Pastors frequently say things like, "My phone begins to ring at six in the morning and doesn't seem to stop until twelve at night." The pastors have become babysitters of the churches, and all the burdens seem to be placed upon them. No single man can handle such a responsibility, and in most cases, a pastor has little opportunity to get to the real work for which he was ordained. Today we develop a few professional evangelists to take the place of the evangelistic work of every pastor.

Because the pastor has a status above everyone else in the church, there is always the danger of deferring to him whether or not he is faithful to the message or to the principles of righteousness. More and more, the pastor becomes a controverted individual within the church. Some are ready to follow him implicitly, irrespective of what he believes or where he leads, while others become burdened when he is unfaithful to his high and holy calling and to God's message.

This has caused laity to fragment and become contentious one with another over the issues. Those who adopt a policy of supporting the pastor irrespective of his faithfulness or unfaithfulness are considered to be loyal and faithful members, while those who cannot support the actions of a pastor leading God's church astray are considered to be the "troublers of Israel." These two segments of the church become hostile one to the other. Often the influence of the pastor has been destroyed as he has taken over the business meetings, the board meetings, and the nominating committees. Too frequently, these pastors are accused of manipulating the nominating committee so that those who support them are chosen for the most influential roles within the church.

Often in decision-making, pastors have exercised so great an influence that laity have been disaffected. An issue as simple as the building of a new church hall has caused grave consequences. The following example is typical. The church members are generally agreed on the building of a fellowship hall; however, they differ in opinion as to the size of the hall. Some want a larger hall, thinking that the church should look to the future and not just build for the present needs. Another significant group believe that the church should not go beyond their means and incur debt. They suggest that a hall be built that can later be expanded as the need arises, but which will suit their present needs. The pastor unwisely throws his not inconsiderable influence on the side of those wanting the larger hall.

The following week comments can be heard among the dissenting members. These include, "It's all right for the pastor to say we need to have a bigger hall; he will not be around when we have to find the money to pay off the debt," or "If these people want a hall that size, they can pay for it. Not a cent of my money is going to go into it." Thus, a church becomes divided, and the pastor's influence is greatly diminished amongst a significant segment of the church. Furthermore, the strong influence of the pastor permits Satan a far greater opportunity to exercise his own influence. It is much easier to control one man's mind than many men's minds.

A pastor is not superhuman. He is like the rest of humanity, fallible before the pressures of Satan. God's method is decentralization; and the present form of church governance has aided and abetted the designs of Satan. Generally speaking, the laity have become inert and passive, and that is precarious for their eternal destiny. The deacons do little more than take up the offering, occasionally do a little busy-bee work around the church, and assist with an ordinance or a baptism. The ministry for which they are called and ordained is never fulfilled.

The same is true of the elders. The responsibility of eldership in many churches has become not much more than a ceremonial post with the elders announcing a hymn, reading announcements, and offering corporate prayer, but in no wise giving the spiritual leadership for which they were ordained.

Finally, by ministers filling roles for which they were not ordained or called, they sometimes go through a whole year without bringing one soul to the Lord. That is not fair to the ministers, for others' respect for them generally drops dramatically as a result of this alteration of roles. It is certainly not fair to the laity, either. We make an earnest plea for our church to return to the pattern that God has ordained.

11

The Saga of the Church Manual

The central role of the Church Manual in Seventh-day Adventist Churches today makes it hard to believe that for almost 90 years, Seventh-day Adventists had no church manual. There was strong opposition in the early days to a church manual, so none was framed. The pioneers of the Seventh-day Adventist Church were adamant that their only basis of faith was the Bible. With clarion tones they declared, "We have no creed but the Bible." "The Bible and the Bible only is our basis of faith and practice." These watch-cries were the basis of the acceptance of all of the great truths of God. The servant of the Lord strongly endorsed this stand.

> The Bible, and the Bible alone, is to be our creed, the sole bond of union; all who bow to this Holy Word will be in harmony (*Selected Messages,* Book 1, p. 416).

It was on the basis of these declarations that the early Adventists proclaimed that the Seventh-day Adventist Church had been raised up in the last days in response to prophetic fulfillment. They used texts such as,

> Here is the patience of the saints: here are they that keep the commandments of God, and the faith of Jesus (Revelation 14:12).

> The dragon was wroth with the woman, and went to make war with the remnant of her seed, which keep the commandments of God, and have the testimony of Jesus Christ (Revelation 12:17).

> Blessed are they that do his commandments, that they may have right to the tree of life, and may enter in through the gates into the city (Revelation 22:14).

In the organization of the General Conference in 1863, no thought was given to the establishment of a creed. Such was considered not only unnecessary, but dangerous to a church. Noting that, like the Roman Catholics, many Protestant churches had chosen to formulate creeds, the Seventh-day Adventists strongly believed that this had brought impotency and formalism to these churches. However, as the Seventh-day Adventist Church grew and expanded, and more and more young men came into the ministry who had not had the opportunity to be part of the formulation of the early Seventh-day Adventist beliefs, there was increasing concern that these men might not have the same clear vision to handle the situations arising in the church, and thus would not give the kind of leadership necessary for the remnant movement. Therefore, there was talk about developing some guidelines by which they could carry on their ministry. A major decision point was reached in 1883, when the General Conference appointed an ad hoc committee to study the concept of developing a Seventh-day Adventist Church Manual. After serious considerations, the ad hoc committee voted unanimously to recommend that no such manual be established in the Seventh-day Adventist Church. Their reasoning was persuasive, and was recorded in the *Review and Herald.*

> It is the unanimous opinion of the committee appointed to consider the matter of a Church Manual, that it would not be advisable to have a Church Manual. We consider it unnecessary because we already have surmounted the greatest difficulties connected with church organization without one; and perfect harmony exists among us on this subject. It would seem to many like a step towards the formation of a creed or a discipline, other than the Bible, something we have always been opposed to as a denomination. If we had one, we fear many, especially these commencing to preach, would study it to obtain guidance in religious matters, rather that to seek it in the Bible, and from the leading of the Spirit of God, which would tend to their hindrance in genuine religious experience and in knowledge of the mind of the Spirit. It was in taking similar steps that other bodies of Christians first began to lose their simplicity and became formal and spiritually lifeless. Why should we imitate them? The committee feels, in short, that our tendency should be in the direction of the policy and close conformity of the Bible, rather than to elaborate defining every point in the church management and church ordinances (*Review and Herald,* Nov. 20, 1883).

Taking up the report of the ad hoc committee, the General Conference voted unanimously to accept the recommendation, and the following week, Elder George Butler, then president of the General Conference, also added persuasive reasons why we should not have a church manual.

> When brethren who have favored a manual have even contended that such a work was not to be anything like a creed or a discipline, or to have any authority to settle disputed points, but was only to be considered as a book containing hints for the help of those of little experience, yet it must be evident that such a work, issued under the auspices of the General Conference, would at once, carry with it much weight of authority, and would be consulted by most of our young ministers. It would gradually shape and mould the entire body; and those who did not follow it would be considered out of harmony with established principles of church order. And really, is this not the object of a manual? What would be the use of one if not to accomplish such a result? But would this result, on a whole, be a benefit? Would our ministers be broader, more original, more self-reliant men? Would they be better depended on in great emergencies? Would their spiritual experience likely be deeper and their judgment more reliable? We think the tendency all the other way. . . . We have preserved simplicity, and have prospered in so doing. It is best to let well enough alone. For these and other reasons, the church manual was rejected. It is probable that it will never be brought forward again (*Review and Herald,* November 27, 1883).

Ironically, it will be noticed that Butler predicted that never again would the issue of a manual be discussed in the Adventist Church. Unfortunately, this prediction was not prophetic, for 49 years later, in 1932, the first Seventh-day Adventist Church Manual was produced. It was as if we wanted to be like the other churches around us, though it meant following the pathway they had already proved would fail. It seemed that we no longer felt that all the principles that we needed were in the Bible and the Spirit of Prophecy. Of course, it would not have been wrong, we believe, to put out a publication which contained all the statements in the

Bible and Spirit of Prophecy relevant to church governance and management. Such would have been useful and profitable, because it would have been wholly built upon the Word of God.

One thing that becomes obvious in hindsight is that the pioneers of the Seventh-day Adventist Church were very perceptive as to what would likely happen if we formulated a church manual. Any Seventh-day Adventist church member who has served for any length of time on a church board or committee probably has seen some, if not all, of the following problems arise. The first problem that may be noticed is that ministers, especially young ones, often turn to the Church Manual as a guide to their ministry rather than directly to Inspiration. This is by no means limited to young ministers; it includes pastors at all levels of their ministerial experience. It also must be noticed that it is not only the ministers, but also many of the laity, who treat the Church Manual almost as if it were inspired, as the very Word of God itself. In doing so, they are limiting their ministry, because they are bound by the notions of men rather than by the direct commands of God.

One cannot help but believe that Elder Butler was correct when he asked the rhetorical questions about whether such a manual would better fit ministers for the work that God had called them to fulfill. There is no question that the manual has proved to be a vehicle that has diminished the effectiveness of the ministry of many of our pastors and lay leaders.

Secondly, the fear has been fulfilled that such a manual would lead to an authoritarian type of situation, and those who under the moving of the Holy Spirit felt impelled to move in a direction contrary to the Church Manual would be perceived as being out of harmony with church order, or even being apostate. Often, the Church Manual is used as a "club" to bring laity and church boards into conformity. The Church Manual is also used as a basis for defining whether men and women are faithful or unfaithful to the Seventh-day Adventist faith. This is a tragic situation.

A third assertion was made that such a manual would lead the church toward credalism, something that early Seventh-day Adventists abhorred as of papal origin. The Twenty-Seven Statements of Fundamental Belief as voted at the Dallas General Conference Session in 1980 are being used by many today as a creed. This will be explored much further in the chapter entitled "Drift Toward Credalism."

The fourth insightful observation made was that organization and all the difficulties associated with it had all been surmounted without the need of a church manual. The pioneers had gone to the Word of God for the basis of these foundational principles. It is interesting to note that Sister White also gave continuing counsel over the years for the organization and administration of the Seventh-day Adventist Church. Sadly we note that as minds moved more toward formalizing the Church Manual, the church tended less and less to follow the divine counsel.

A fifth problem Elder Butler quite rightly pointed out was that even if a manual was considered only to be made up of suggestions with no authority, the fact that it was put out under the auspices of the General Conference would give it much weight. Surely, that is true. This undue prestige becomes even more obvious when one has worked in non-Western countries as both authors have. In some of these places the Church Manual is treated with a reverence which puts it virtually on the same level as the Bible and the Spirit of Prophecy. It sometimes appears to be treated as having greater authority, at least in some matters.

It must be pointed out that before the 1932 Church Manual was published, there had been a number of attempts by various leaders to set up guidelines and principles. Some of these became the forerunners of principles that are in the Church Manual today. Naturally, they did not have the authority that a General Conference-produced Church Manual had. However, even those might have been going too far.

Today there are those who are victims, not only of arbitrary, but also of erratic use of the Church Manual. From time to time, we hear claims from laity that pastors are using the Church Manual when it is favorable to their wishes and desires, and ignoring it when they want to move in another direction.

A classic example has been reported from the West Coast of the United States. In a certain church there, the nominating committee made a decision that did not meet the approval of the church pastor. Quite illegally, according to the Church Manual, the pastor refused to allow the nominating committee report to go before the church, but decided that it must be reviewed before the church board. When the meeting was held, it was discovered that two men from the conference were there to assist the pastor in his efforts to derail the decision of the nominating committee. For over an hour the board and those present from the nominating committee debated the issue of the right of the board to review the nominating committee's report. In the end, it was stated that, though it was not consistent with the "letter" of the Church Manual, it was consistent with the intent of the Church Manual. On this highly tenuous premise, the board voted to refer the nominating committee report back, asking the members to follow the direction of the Church Manual as it was interpreted by the board. (As can be readily perceived, such lack of logic and consistency did not inspire a favorable response from some of the members of the nominating committee; a number of them resigned.)

Since 1932 the Church Manual has been revised every General Conference Session. The changes that are made are often significant both in number and in content. We have in our possession the 1932 Manual and the 1990 Manual. One does not have to compare the two for very long to realize the dramatic changes that have taken place in the 58-year period between the formation of the first Church Manual and the 1990 Church Manual. It is only to be expected that further divergence will come as long as there are General Conference Sessions to revise and modify the Church Manual.

Some of these changes will come into sharp focus when we deal with other issues such as fundamental beliefs of the Seventh-day Adventist Church, grounds for disfellowshiping, and the changes in the baptismal vows. It is our evaluation that these changes overwhelmingly have not been for the profit of the church, but are leading more in the fashion of the fallen churches of the world and in the direction of greater control over the laity. The very fact that there are so many changes each quinquennium is positive proof that the Church Manual is a document of human devising, and therefore not without significant danger.

One thing is clear to long-term members of the Seventh-day Adventist Church: the establishment of the Church Manual has not increased the spirituality of the members nor the effectiveness of the ministry. It is our recommendation that we put the Church

Manual aside and do what the pioneers of the Seventh-day Adventist Church did—go back to the Bible and the Spirit of Prophecy for our guidance in church governance.

12

The Drift Toward Credalism

Theपioneers of the Seventh-day Adventist Church fought fiercely against credalism. They rightly saw that the production of a creed would lead to sterility in the church, to formalism and persecution. These pioneers had carefully studied the history of the Christian church, and were fully aware of these hazards.

In volume three of *Spiritual Gifts,* we have a clear statement of the rejection of credalism in the early Seventh-day Adventist ranks.

> The gifts have been superseded in the popular churches by human creeds. The object of the gifts, as stated by Paul, was "for the perfecting of the saints, for the work of the ministry, for the edifying of the body of Christ, till we all come in the unity of the faith." These were Heaven's appointed means to secure the unity of the church. Christ prayed that his people might be one, as he was one with his Father. Read John xvii. Paul exhorted the Corinthians in the name of Christ to be perfectly joined together in the same mind, and in the same judgment. Read 1 Cor. i, 10; Rom. xv, 5; Phil. ii, 1, 2; 1 Pet. iii, 8; v, 5. The gifts were given to secure this state of unity.

> But the popular churches have introduced another means of preserving unity, namely, human creeds. These creeds secure a sort of unity to each denomination; but they have all proved inefficient, as appears from the "New Schools" and "Reformed" of almost every creed-bound denomination under heaven. Hence the many kinds of Baptists, of Presbyterians, and of Methodists, &c., &c. (*Spiritual Gifts,* vol. 3, p. 29).

It is important to notice that these statements were made in 1864. The danger of credalism was thoroughly understood, and formed the basis of strong opposition in our church to the credal form. The above statements point out that the very purpose of the creed is to preserve unity, but in reality such creeds have failed to do so: in all churches with creeds there has been much evidence of division. There is only one way to retain unity, and that is by perfect obedience to the Word of God through the power of the indwelling Christ.

No one pointed out the danger of credalism and its direction better than J. N. Loughborough. Loughborough detailed five stages in the maturing of credalism:

Stage One: The statements of belief are used only to help those not of the faith to understand what the believers teach. At this stage, there is no basis upon which the members of the church are bound by such a statement.

Stage Two: The statements of belief are used as a basis for preparing candidates for baptism and for church membership. At this stage, of course, the statements of belief carry some weight of authority, though only for those who are preparing for membership within the church.

Stage Three: The statements of belief become the standard of orthodoxy. Now the church accepts these statements of belief as an unchanging and rigid definition of not only what are standard beliefs, but what are the expected beliefs of all members.

Stage Four: The statements of belief are used as a basis of church discipline, and failure to acknowledge certain beliefs can lead to church censure, or, ultimately, church disfellowshipment (or excommunication).

Stage Five: The statements of belief are held to be so critical that if anyone disagrees, they face not only disfellowshipment (or even excommunication), but they also face persecution that in times past has led to imprisonment and martyrdom.

Loughborough's insightful presentation of the development of credalism surely raises alarm in the minds of perceptive Seventh-day Adventists. As we will demonstrate, the Seventh-day Adventist Church has reached at least Stage Four, and there are those who say that we are at the beginning of Stage Five. Let us examine the development.

In 1872 the Seventh-day Adventist Church published, on the steam press at Battle Creek, Michigan, "*A Declaration of the Fundamental Principles Taught and Practiced by the Seventh-day Adventists.*" (See Appendix A.) It will be noticed that the list was not called "fundamental beliefs," but simply "fundamental principles." The authors went to great pains to make sure that the twenty-five statements incorporated in these fundamental principles had no weight of authority whatever concerning the members of the church. Indeed, this fitted precisely into Loughborough's Stage One of the development of credalism. In their efforts to make it clear that this had not the slightest impact upon membership in the church, they placed this disclaimer,

> In presenting to the public the synopsis of the faith, we wish to have it distinctly understood that we have no articles of faith, creed, or discipline, aside from the Bible. We do not put forth this as having any authority with our people, nor is it designed to secure uniformity among them, as a system of faith, but it is a brief statement of what is, and has been, with great unanimity, held by them (*Declaration of Fundamental Principles, Taught and Practiced by Seventh-day Adventists*).

This statement could not more perfectly reflect the Stage One intention of the development of credalism. The authors have discovered that many faithful Adventists have been thrilled as they have read through the twenty-five statements in the Declaration of Principles given in 1872. Indeed, our hearts have been warmed by the certainty of faith expressed on such issues as the fallen nature of Jesus, the completion of the atonement in the second apartment of the heavenly sanctuary, and the imminent return of Jesus. The Declaration calls for full victory in the life under the power of Jesus Christ, strongly affirms the sanctuary message and the importance of 1844, upholds the commandments of God, and makes clear statements on the centrality of the Sabbath at the end of time. It pinpoints the Papacy as the man of sin of Biblical prophecy, and plainly defines the Millennium and the state of the dead.

Nevertheless, we have to hesitate in a full approval of such a document, because without this first document, we would not be in the position as a church that we are in today. We do not know whether such a statement subsequently may have been used for the preparation of candidates for entrance into the church. However, it is of grave significance to note that sixty years later, in 1932, with the advent of the first Church Manual, the statements presented were treated altogether differently than those in the statement of fundamental principles printed in 1872. Twenty-two statements of belief were defined in the first Church Manual. No longer, it will be noticed, were they called fundamental principles; they were simply called fundamental beliefs of Seventh-day Adventists. There was also no disclaimer as was found in the 1872 list of fundamental principles. Before giving the Twenty-Two Statements, the simple preamble said,

Seventh-day Adventists have certain fundamental beliefs, the principle features of which, together with a portion of the Scripture reference upon which they are based, may be summarized as follows (*Seventh-day Adventist Church Manual,* 1932 edition, p. 180).

It will be noted that by 1932, we had reached Stage Three of Loughborough's development of a creed—orthodoxy. They were now the "fundamental beliefs" of Seventh-day Adventists. Reading through these twenty-two fundamental beliefs, they still ring with a high level of authenticity in terms of what Seventh-day Adventists as a whole believe (See appendix B).

For those who have been members of the Seventh-day Adventist Church for many years, it will be recalled that these fundamental beliefs were once hardly mentioned. They seemed to carry very little weight, and certainly were not used in the more objectionable form of credalism. However, a great change came in 1980. After years of study and preparation, a recommendation was brought to the General Conference Session in Dallas, Texas, advising the adoption of a new set of beliefs, also called "Fundamental Beliefs of Seventh-day Adventists." These were suggested to the assembled delegates as a replacement for the older vows that had been formerly presented to the church.

There were some present who saw the danger of these vows. One was Dr. Ralph Larson. Dr. Larson was not an accredited delegate to the 1980 General Conference Session, but he had asked his union president if, as a visitor to the session, he would have permission to speak to the motion. It was indicated to him that this would be quite appropriate. Dr. Larson's main thrust was to ask that further time be spent, especially because of the concerns over a few of the statements. He, unfortunately, in the emotion of the situation, moved (which, as a non-delegate, he could not do) that the statements be referred back for further study over the next five years. This created what was probably one of the most tense interchanges ever witnessed at a General

Conference Session. Indeed, so unfortunate was the incident that the delegates later voted to expunge from the record the events that had taken place.

The delegates voted for the new statements of belief. For some reason, unlike previous statements of belief, these began to have considerable weight of authority among the members of the Seventh-day Adventist Church. They not only began to be used to define orthodoxy, but increasingly also began to be used as a basis of church discipline.

Before looking into that aspect, however, it is important to note that there are some very serious concerns relevant to these beliefs. Statement Two uses the troubling term "the Trinity." Ellen White avoided this phrase, using instead the term "the Godhead," no doubt recognizing that the concept of the Trinity as presented in the mysteries of Catholicism is not consistent with Seventh-day Adventism. Furthermore, Statement Four, "The Son," is carefully worded. While His divine and human nature are confirmed, there is a studied effort to avoid defining whether Christ, in His humanity, took upon Himself the nature of sinful man or the nature of sinless man. This leaves open the option of dualism within the Seventh-day Adventist Church. This has confused many into believing that, since the church has not taken a stand on this issue, we can believe either way, or even in a third way, that Christ in some ways took upon Himself fallen nature, and in other ways unfallen nature. A typical interpretation of that alternative was voted by the British Union Conference, March 5, 1986.

> Whereas the Seventh-day Adventist Church has not issued a definitive statement on the post- or pre-fallen nature of Christ, thus accommodating alternative viewpoints and, whereas there are groups within the British Union who teach one particular viewpoint as the only valid position, the British Union Conference endorses the official position of the church which allows for a validity of a dual interpretation of the nature of Christ (British Union Conference Minutes, March 5, 1986).

The concept that He took partly fallen and partly unfallen nature was advanced in the special tithe supplement produced by Roger W. Coon, Associate Secretary of the Ellen G. White Estate, inserted in the North American issues of the *Adventist Review*, November 1991. It said,

> He took a nature that in certain respects was like Adam's before the fall, but in other respects was like Adam after the fall (*Adventist Review*, Supplement on Tithe, November, 1991).

It has been the experience of the authors that lack of clarity in the statements of belief is not consistent with the clear testimony of Scripture and the Spirit of Prophecy.

> Letters have been coming in to me, affirming that Christ could not have had the same nature as man, for if He had, He would have fallen under similar temptations. If He did not have man's nature, He could not be our example. If He was not a partaker of our nature, He could not have been tempted as man has been (*Selected Messages*, vol. 1, p. 408).

> The great work of redemption could be carried out only by the Redeemer taking the place of fallen Adam (*Review and Herald*, February 24, 1874).

> It was in the order of God that Christ should take upon Himself the form and nature of fallen man, that He might be made perfect through suffering, and endure Himself the strength of Satan's temptations, that He might the better know how to succor those who should be tempted (*Spiritual Gifts*, vol. 4, p. 115).

> He took upon His sinless nature our sinful nature, that He might know how to succor those that are tempted (*Medical Ministry*, p. 181).

Sad to say, there is much ambivalence and resistance toward those who believe the clear Biblical and Spirit of Prophecy declarations on Christ's nature. There are also problems in Statement Twenty-One, dealing with Christian behavior, which, while excellent in many ways, falls short of the day-by-day victory promised to us through the power of the indwelling Christ.

Another area of deep concern revolves around Statement Twenty-Three, which addresses Christ's ministry in the heavenly sanctuary. There it is stated:

> In it Christ ministers on our behalf, making available to believers the benefits of His atoning sacrifice offered once for all on the cross.

This is the kind of statement that was used back in the mid-1950's to placate the evangelical leaders who would not accept the fact that the final atonement is made in the heavenly sanctuary.

That the framer of the 1980 *Statement of Beliefs* deliberately left a number of issues (specifically, victorious Christian living, the human nature of Christ, and the atonement) vague is confirmed by the leaders of the North American Division in the insert in the November 5, 1992 *Adventist Review* entitled "Issues—The Seventh-day Adventist Church & Certain Private Organizations," page 8. What an incredible admission!

It has been our observation that the statements of belief voted in 1932, and variations since, did not take upon themselves the role of a creed. However, an entirely new situation has arisen with the Twenty-Seven Statements voted in during the 1980 Dallas General Conference Session. They are being used as a basis for church discipline, the fourth stage of the development of credalism. Here is an alarming trend for a church that stands four-square on the Bible as its only basis of faith and practice, and strongly espouses the principles of religious liberty.

A typical example comes from the Bury-St. Edmonds Church in East Anglia, England. This church, formed from a company in 1991, barred a number of faithful Adventists from membership because they refused to sign a document which included this statement: "I promise to support the doctrines and beliefs of the church as outlined in the Twenty-Seven Fundamental Beliefs." Some faithful Adventists resolutely refused to sign such a document, and rightly so. Because they refused, they were not allowed to become foundation members of the church.

One cannot escape the clear evidence that many within the Seventh-day Adventist Church are moving toward credalism. On one occasion, the then-pastor of the church of which Colin is a member asked him what statements of belief he was expected to teach. Though it is not well known, in the 1990 Church Manual (and several others before it), there have been two statements of belief, and he had been using "Fundamental Beliefs of Seventh-day Adventists" as voted at the 1980 General Conference Session, which appears on pages 23-31. However, toward the back of the manual on pages 179-182 is the other statement of beliefs, entitled, "Outline of Doctrinal Beliefs." In this set of statements, twenty-eight beliefs are enunciated. Colin's answer to the pastor was, "Use neither; just use the Bible." This, we believe, is the soundest counsel that we can give to pastors and laity alike.

13

What Has Happened to Our Baptismal Vows?

Before entering into the sacred rite of baptism, it has ever been the custom of Christians to affirm the faith into which they are being baptized. This public declaration is a basis upon which decisions are made for new members to be voted into the fellowship of the church. One well-known example of this is the experience of the Ethiopian eunuch. The eunuch asked,

> See, here is water; what doth hinder me to be baptized? (Acts 8:36.)

Philip responded,

> If thou believest with all thine heart, thou mayest. And he answered and said, I believe that Jesus Christ is the Son of God (Acts 8:37).

The present truth for that time was the acceptance of Christ as the Son of God. This belief incorporated not only His divine origin, but also His death, sacrifice, and ministry for mankind. In the development of the Seventh-day Adventist Church it has likewise been accepted practice to have candidates for baptism publicly declare their allegiance to the great truths encompassed in the Adventist message.

It will be immediately noticed that the vows that are taken should have much to do with the Christian commitment that a man or woman has made. In earlier times, there was a thorough investigation of the candidates for baptism in front of the congregation of the church, so that it might be ascertained whether or not they were ready for baptism and the heavy responsibility of church membership. In an age where most Christians have forgotten the great truths of the gospel, it has become increasingly important that the candidates affirm the great central themes of Adventism, as well as the lifestyle that the Bible outlines. An alarming situation now exists, in which the baptismal vows have been so eroded that many of the great truths have been lost.

In the 1932 *Church Manual* there were twenty-one suggested vows for the examination of baptismal candidates. A later guideline that Elder Joe Crews of Amazing Facts has used since he began his ministry in 1946 also has very strong principles for the examination of candidates, though they are only fifteen in number. However, a very cursory look at the baptismal vows that have been listed in the *Church Manual* for many years shows a dangerous diminution and down-playing of some of the key commitments that Adventists of former generations declared.

The vows affirmed are one way that the congregation can ascertain whether or not prospective members understand the great truths of the Seventh-day Adventist faith. Upon this they can make an evaluation of whether or not this man or woman is ready to bear the heavy responsibility of the remnant at the end of time. With the tremendous pressure presently upon pastors to gain numbers in the church, there is a concomitant risk that such pastors, in their endeavor to meet the expectations of church leaders, and perhaps their own ambition, will find it very easy to baptize people who have only a passing knowledge of the great Advent Message.

The acceptance of men and women into church fellowship is not a minor matter. Indeed, it is a matter that should involve the earnest effort of all the faithful members of the church. We are too close to the end of time to bring members into the church, either by baptism or by transfer of membership, without being certain that they are men and women who love the Lord and who will stretch every energy to forward the cause of the kingdom of heaven.

Some have held that it is not important that the vows no longer have the strength that they once had. After all, it is possible for the candidates to carefully go through the Twenty-seven Fundamental Beliefs. However, it is the observation of the authors that many have come into the church with little or no knowledge of some of the most critical aspects of the truth. Colin recalls a number of such incidents.

One day he was preaching in a church in northern Maryland on the Investigative Judgment. After the service he heard a woman speaking very strongly to the pastor, and the indications were that she had been very unhappy with his sermon. When Colin approached the pastor, the pastor said everything was all right now, the woman had thought that he had preached some newfangled heresy. When Colin sat by her during the fellowship dinner after the Sabbath service, he raised the issue to her, and she indicated that all was well; the pastor had assured her that what Colin had preached had been valid Adventism. Colin asked the woman how long she had been a member of the Seventh-day Adventist Church. He was shocked to learn that she had been baptized in Texas fifteen years before. Apparently, in those fifteen years in the church, she had heard no preaching of that message, nor had she been introduced to it before she was baptized. That was a tragic situation, but hardly an isolated one.

More recently, Colin preached in Singapore on the Investigative Judgment. A family that had been Adventist for five years, thrilled by the message, told him they had never heard it before.

There are other areas of vital truth being neglected, as well. In dialogue with some folk who had been brought into the Seventh-day Adventist Church in an evangelistic crusade in California, Colin was told that not even the name of Ellen White had been mentioned before they were baptized with sixty-plus other candidates. Not very long after their baptism it was Spirit of Prophecy Day, and apparently the speaker gave a strong presentation on the role of the Spirit of Prophecy in the remnant church. These people were totally taken aback. They wondered if they had been deceived and delivered into a cult. By the grace of God, they did not leave, as others did, but decided to study it through, and today are strong believers in the prophetic gift of Ellen White. However, it is hardly surprising that they represent only a handful of those sixty-some who were baptized, who are still faithful members of the Seventh-day Adventist Church.

While it is not here possible to point out all the limitations and deletions in the present baptismal vows when compared to those of former years, it is possible to make the comparisons in appendixes C, D, and E. However, we want to share with you some of the major deletions and changes in the baptismal vows. First, let us look at the issue of the Spirit of Prophecy.

In the 1932 *Church Manual*, Belief Eighteen reads, "Do you believe the Bible doctrine of "spiritual gifts" in the church, and do you believe in the gift of the Spirit of Prophecy which has been manifested in the remnant in the ministry and writings of Mrs. E. G. White?"

Compare this with Number Eight in the 1990 baptismal vows. "Do you accept the Bible teaching of spiritual gifts and believe that the gift of prophecy is one of the identifying marks of the remnant church?" The perceptive reader will notice that the name of Sister White is not mentioned in the 1990 vows. It would be possible for any Pentecostal, Baptist, or member of another previous persuasion to say amen to this without any knowledge of what is meant by the prophetic gift. This leaves opportunity for pastors, desperate for numbers, or hurrying to prepare people for baptism, to ignore one of the most vital truths identifying the remnant.

There is another interesting difference between these statements. Whereas the 1932 list refers to the Spirit of Prophecy, the 1990 version refers to the gift of prophecy. The *gift* of prophecy is not the identifying mark of the remnant church: it is the *Spirit* of Prophecy, as will be confirmed by Revelation 12:17 and Revelation 19:10.

Another concern we have is the temperance vow. We want to compare this with the set of vows that Elder Crews shared with us from 1946. Number Nine asks, "Is it your purpose to obey the command to eat and drink to the glory of God (1 Cor. 10:31) by abstaining from all intoxicating liquors (Prov. 23:29-32), tobacco in all its forms (1 Cor. 3:16, 17), swine's flesh (Isa. 66:15, 17), narcotics, tea, coffee, and other harmful things?" Now let us review what is said in the vows in the 1990 *Church Manual*, Number Ten. We hasten to point out that we far prefer the lead into this vow, for it does state the underlying principle; however, we are burdened by the deletions. "Do you believe that your body is the temple of the Holy Spirit; and will you honor God by caring for it, avoiding the use of that which is harmful; abstaining from all unclean foods; from the use, manufacture, or sale of alcoholic beverages; the use, manufacture, or sale of tobacco in any of its forms for human consumption; and from the misuse of or trafficking in narcotics or other drugs?"

There are some things in the 1990 vow we prefer. It does not limit unclean foods to swine's flesh. It adds the modern-day problems of trafficking in narcotics and other drugs, and it certainly includes the manufacture or sale of these harmful substances; however, it neglects to include tea and coffee.

In 1991, Colin was preparing a sizable group for baptism. When he read the vows that included tea and coffee, one man decided that he would not be baptized because he was still apparently a coffee user. When he spoke to his sister, who was a Seventh-day Adventist, she said, "Well, he is only saying that because he is part of a health institution." Yet the Servant of the Lord has declared that drinking tea and coffee is a sin.

> Tea and coffee drinking is a sin, an injurious indulgence, which, like other evils, injures the soul (*Counsels on Diets and Foods,* p. 425).

Regrettably, the man stated, "I think I'll get the pastor to baptize me in the church that I attend. I don't think he will make an issue of coffee." We certainly pray that his pastor did make an issue of that which the Lord has designated as sin.

We are burdened in an even greater way by some of the vows that are left out. For example, Number Thirteen of the 1932 *Church Manual* reads, "Do you believe that we are living in the time of the Investigative Judgment, which began in 1844, and that Christ, as our High Priest, is closing His ministry in the most holy apartment of the heavenly sanctuary in preparation for His coming?"

We have searched through the thirteen vows contained in the 1990 *Church Manual* in vain to find any vow that even slightly sounds like this one. In the light of the experiences of Colin in respect to the Investigative Judgment, it is clear that this vow certainly needs to be included in any statements of belief. After all, the Investigative Judgment is part of the great sanctuary truth which the servant of the Lord has told us is the foundation of our faith.

> The correct understanding of the ministration in the heavenly sanctuary is the foundation of our faith (*Evangelism,* p. 221).

Especially burdensome to the authors is the fact that there is little emphasis upon the high standards of God's church. Two stand out strikingly: the standards related to Christian dress and Christian recreation. The vows shared with us by Elder Joe Crews on these vital issues are especially powerful. Number Ten asks, "Are you willing to follow the Bible rule of modesty and simplicity of dress, refraining from the wearing of earrings, necklaces, bracelets, beads, rings, etc., and from any lack of dress that is out of keeping with the Bible rule of modesty? 1 Tim. 2:9, 10; 1 Peter 3:3, 4; Ex. 33:5, 6; Gen. 35:2-4." Number Twelve inquires, "Is it your purpose to come out from the world and be separate in obedience to God's command in 2 Corinthians 6:17, by refraining from following the sinful practices of the world, such as dancing, card-playing, theater-going, novel-reading, etc. and by shunning all questionable worldly amusements? 1 John 2:15; James 1:27, 4:4." The 1932 *Church Manual* also has strong statements on both of these; Number Seventeen deals with the matter of dress, and Number Twenty with the issue of amusements.

With the terrible erosion of dress standards in God's church and the avalanche of entertainment, sports, and other amusements in our ranks, surely these principles need to be taught, understood and accepted by all who are asking to come into the membership of God's remnant church. Some might hasten to say that these standards are too high, but how can they be when they are God's standards? We are not bringing members into a club or a society; we are bringing them into the remnant church of prophecy, the church that God has called to be without "spot, or wrinkle, or any such thing" (Ephesians 5:27). God is looking for a pure church, a church that is holy, that is separate from the world. Let us put away the tantalizing deceptions that Satan has for this generation. These are not man's standards; these are God's standards. We have no authority to in any way change them or delete from them.

We suspect that one of the main reasons why these standards have been dropped is embarrassment for the fact that so many of our people are now engaging in worldly amusements, and dressing more and more like the world. It is our belief, however, that this is the time to come up to the highest standards that God has ordained. Part of the problem, no doubt, is that we are now up to the third, fourth, and fifth generations of Seventh-day Adventists, and many parents, anxious to have their children baptized, are willing to accept the lowest denominator possible so that their children might have what is deemed to be the security of membership in God's remnant church. That is a shallow view, for obviously, being a member of the church is meaningless if it does not also fully incorporate the standards that God has set for this church.

Many say that high standards will drive our young people away. Surely the evidence is in the other direction. The worldly amusements, worldly standards, lack of challenge to the highest goals that God has set for young people—these diversions are driving our youth away, to the extent that, in North America, approximately three out of every four are leaving the church. A considerable number even of those who remain in the church give overt evidence that they are not trulyx converted.

The authors of this book have made a covenant with the Lord not to baptize anyone into the emaciated standards of the present baptismal vows. Rather, we prepare and ask reformation according to the whole standards of the baptismal vows. Of course, such Biblical standards are presented in the light of the matchless love revealed in Calvary. We call upon every minister to take such an approach, and exhort every layman preparing candidates for baptism to make sure that, from all they can ascertain, their candidates are ready to accept all the responsibilities that church membership holds for them.

14
Church Property Ownership

Contrary to what most pastors and laymen understand, there is no compelling reason why the houses of worship should be owned by the denomination's legal corporation. Some of our readers will no doubt be surprised to learn that, at one time, the church titles were commonly held by the church congregations (usually by a board of trustees who held the title on behalf of the church body). Our experience as lads in Australia has helped to shape our understanding. The Hamilton, Newcastle Church of our youth was owned and administered by the church with a board of five trustees, each trustee a faithful member of the congregation.

There is little doubt that the beginnings of change were motivated by honorable concerns. Those concerns revolved around the possibility that these churches, in the hands of a few lay people, could be wrested from the Seventh-day Adventist Church should there be apostasy of any magnitude among the leaders. Obviously, the change to organizational ownership of the church properties had come to North America earlier than in the late 1940s. In our first *Church Manual* of 1932, there was a major statement on the ownership of church properties which indicated that many properties were in the hands of the denomination at that time; apparently, some were not.

> *Title to church properties.*—A. All our church properties should be held by the conference corporations. This is the only means of insuring the continuous use of denominational property. This method prevents a few individuals who may become disaffected, from diverting from the Seventh-day Adventist body, property which belongs to the denomination. In the history of this movement no case is recorded of a property being wrongfully diverted where held by the conference corporation. In order to safeguard denominational property, whether real or personal, it is necessary to have the title vested in a corporation created by a conference organization

according to the laws governing in the locality where the property is located (*Church Manual,* 1932 Edition, p. 105, 106).

Having read this statement in more recent times, we have been surprised at how closely such arguments were reflected in the changes that came into Australia in the late 1940s. The authors were in their early- to mid-teens when these events took place. A special board meeting had been called at the Hamilton Church, where representation was made from the conference to the board, urging that the property title of the Hamilton Church be placed with the Australasian Conference Association (ACA), the legal body of the church in Australia and New Zealand. As indicated in the 1932 *Church Manual,* the arguments from the conference revolved around the fact that it would be possible for a small number of men to apostatize, by which we could very well lose the church. If the church was owned by the conference association, however, it would be secure and in no risk of ever being lost. Though we were still relatively young, we could perceive very quickly that our father favored the change. In fact, we recall him indicating that it was seemingly only the trustees themselves and their relatives who had any opposition to this. We suppose it could have been assumed by the other church members that it was a self-serving opposition. The decision to place this church and other churches under the umbrella of the denomination seemed wise and prudent, and such was voted. Nevertheless, the decision to place ownership of our church in the hands of the conference did not come easily. This change could only be effected under New South Wales law on the basis of a 75 percent majority. It took more than one meeting to achieve this result. No doubt the same decisions were made by many other churches around the divisions.

However, what was prudent in the late 1940s may not necessarily be prudent today. Church members need to take a second look at this situation. Once the churches are owned by the conference, it possesses total discretionary power. While it is true that in most cases the conferences have worked smoothly with the issues and desires of the church, increasingly, conflicts are arising. It has become apparent that if a church decides to move in a direction contrary to the counsel of the conference, as is its right, the conference can, and sometimes does, lock the doors of the church. Colin well remembers passing a neat church in southern Washington state which had been padlocked by the conference. To Colin this was an extraordinary situation. While he did not know the reason that the conference took this action, it could be seen that such an act would have a negative effect upon the little community in which that church was located. Another light had gone out.

With ownership of the church building in the hands of the conference, there is increased danger of punitive action being taken against the church community, especially against small churches that have little "political clout." While a conference committee cannot vote to disband a church community, it can, because of its ownership of the building, padlock the church facility. More and more questions arise as to the legality of such an action, and the answer may vary from community to community.

It has been reported in recent times that an Episcopal Church parish in Texas has defected to the Roman Catholic Church. It received the legal go-ahead to transfer all the real property to the Roman Catholic Church.

The case of a Samoan Seventh-day Adventist Church in Auckland, New Zealand, demands examination. We do not understand all the details of the dispute between the church and the North New Zealand Conference. Nevertheless, the broad details are well known. The conference appointed a pastor who was deemed unacceptable by the church community. No amount of negotiation between the church and the conference solved the situation, and the church members refused to accept the designated pastor, choosing their own pastor. The conference padlocked the doors of the church. From personal testimonies we have learned that the lock was removed, presumably by one or more members, who replaced it with their own lock. The conference leaders in turn removed this lock and replaced it with their lock. In the end, pitifully, the whole issue was placed before the court, though that action was clearly contrary to God's Word (see I Corinthians 6). The court ruled in favor of the congregation, and today there is an independent Seventh-day Adventist congregation of Samoan believers in Auckland, New Zealand.

It is now considered necessary to have the property of each church in the hands of the denominational corporation. Any congregation that refuses to do so is in very serious danger of losing recognition by the conference. A classic example is the Marshall Company in North Carolina. The members of that company built their church and paid for it. They wisely decided that in the uncertainties of the present situation they would not surrender the title of the church to the Carolina Conference. In totally unreasonable response, the conference decided that there had been an act of distrust, and refused to recognize the company.

While we believe that it is in the right of church communities to decide to entrust the title of their church to the conference corporation, we also firmly hold that the local churches have the right to choose to retain the title of their church which they have built with their own funds.

A number of years ago Colin was talking with a brother who was very burdened over his experience with his church. Some years earlier a new church had been built. This brother said that he had put $50,000 into the building of the church, and that for the best part of eighteen months he had spent almost every Sunday helping in the construction of the church. Now he said, "I can't even hear truth from the pulpit of my church." His pastor did not preach present truth, and when the congregation sought to invite a speaker who did preach the straight testimony, usurped conference authority forbade this. This type of situation has become increasingly common in our churches.

Some time ago Colin was talking with our father and reminding him of the situation in the late 1940s that led to the decision to place our local church in the hands of the church corporation. In the course of the dialogue Colin asked, "What would you do now?" After some thought, he responded, "I think I would now vote to keep it in the local church trusteeship." As we discussed the issue, we agreed that at the time the decision was made to place our church in the hands of the Australasian Conference Association, there was not the slightest thought that it was possible that the whole conference committee could apostatize; yet today that is a real fear of many Seventh-day Adventists. Many now recognize that a conference committee or officers of a conference may apostatize.

One recent example of the very peril of placing ownership of our churches in conference corporation occurred in the Lake Region Conference. In an effort to support the purchase of a supermarket, the largest black church in the conference (located in Chicago) was offered as a mortgage for the project, unbeknown to the congregation. This project failed. Even if the project had succeeded, that was a totally irresponsible act on the part of conference leadership.

A deeper concern is that, in some conferences, few of the ministers are loyal to the authentic Seventh-day Adventist message. By default, the churches are being taken over by those who are not good representatives of the everlasting gospel which God has given to this people, not only to know, but to believe, to live and to proclaim.

These problems are causing increasingly deep alarm among faithful Seventh-day Adventists, and questions are being raised. Colin was talking to the senior elder of a church that was about to vote the building of a new church facility. The senior elder adamantly asserted that he would do everything possible to encourage the church not to surrender the title of the new church building to the local conference. Such a move would hardly have been considered a few years ago, but it is increasingly becoming part of the thinking of God's faithful flock today, and with valid reasons.

There is another issue of deep concern relevant to the issue of church ownership. Evidence points to the fact that the structure of the Seventh-day Adventist Church now in existence places the whole of the real estate property of the church in danger, should bankruptcy be filed. This fact became obvious when on November 25, 1991, the law firm of Katten, Muchin and Zabis filed a suit against the General Conference of Seventh-day Adventists and the Lake Union Conference of Seventh-day Adventists. The suit alleged default of payment for services rendered to Adventist Living Centers by Katten, Muchin, and Zabis of $321,175.03. (Adventist Living Centers is a Wisconsin-based non-profit corporation headquartered in Warrenville, Illinois.) Apparently, Adventist Living Centers had fallen into financial difficulties and had previously filed for Chapter Eleven bankruptcy. The law firm went to considerable lengths to demonstrate that Adventist Living Centers was an integral part of the Seventh-day Adventist Church, and therefore the General Conference was ultimately responsible for the debt. The affidavit claimed, after providing certain facts, that "The following facts established, and defendants are estopped from denying, that ALC [Adventist Living Centers] also is part of a single, unified Seventh-day Adventist Church; is controlled by the church; is a mere instrumentality of the church; and is the alter ego of the church." They offered many evidences to show that ALC is inextricably part of the church and therefore the General Conference is responsible for the debt and any interest accrued on the debt. If this suit against ALC is sustained in the courts, it is possible that others will follow, and tens of millions of church dollars will be placed in jeopardy.

A side issue to this lawsuit was the untoward way in which the plaintiffs used the Proctor versus General Conference of Seventh-day Adventists case of 1986. In this case, the General Conference sued Derek Proctor, a teacher at Andrews University, who had established a book store and was markedly undercutting the prices for books from the Review and Herald and Pacific Press Publishing Associations. The General Conference won the case, largely on the assertion that next to the Roman Catholic Church the Seventh-day Adventist Church is the most hierarchically organized church in the United States. That decision and that testimony are coming back to haunt us, as now, in a legal battle from the opposite perspective, those suing the General Conference are claiming that judgment as clear proof that the General Conference is responsible for the debts of ALC.

There are many who are deeply concerned about the large debts that are accumulating. Paramount amongst debtors are the hospitals operated under the banner of the Seventh-day Adventist Church. While we are not certain of the present debts, they were quoted in the *Adventist Review* in 1987 as being 2.2 billion dollars, a sum that would certainly bankrupt our church. Should this happen, the question arises, "What would happen to our churches?" Surely, since they are owned by our conferences, they would be sold as disposable assets in order to meet the settlement.

Not only are there the serious debts of the hospitals, but there are also the major debts of our educational institutions. This has led General Conference leadership to call for the closing of at least five of our senior colleges before being forced to close them through irreversible debt.

Furthermore, in October, 1991, it was revealed that the Review and Herald Publishing Association had 5.7 million dollars in long-term debt, and that the board of directors had authorized the borrowing of up to 2.5 million dollars for operational needs. With debts of that magnitude within our church, many are advocating that the church buildings be returned to the local church communities. Should there be a major collapse of our other institutions, there would be a far greater likelihood of retaining the churches if they were not held by the denominational corporation. As things stand at present, a financial collapse would force the denomination into a bankruptcy settlement that could very well encompass every church property that we own in the United States.

The collapse of one institution leading to the failure of another in a domino effect is not a mere hypothetical assertion. In 1991, the bankruptcy of the church's Danish health food company, Nutena, led to the closure of our 90-year-old health facility, the renowned Skodsberg Sanitarium.

We believe that one matter is certain: the time has come for an honest review of the policy that virtually demands that churches surrender the deeds of their property to the conference corporation. We believe that it would be prudent to give all local churches the opportunity again to decide whether they want to leave their church property in the hands of conference legal corporations, or accept the title deeds back into the ownership of their local church communities. We contend that such a move, though painful and difficult, would nonetheless be seen very positively by the laity, and we are confident that the laity would handle the situation with great sincerity and responsibility, as they did for many decades before the church properties were uniformly placed in the hands of local conferences.

15

The Arm of Flesh

For most of its history, the Seventh-day Adventist Church has recognized that, according to Scripture, Christians do not have the right to use the secular courts of law to solve matters that are of an internal nature. For true-hearted Christians, this text has solved the issue:

> Dare any of you, having a matter against another, go to law before the unjust, and not before the saints? Do ye not know that the saints shall judge the world? and if the world shall be judged by you, are ye unworthy to judge the smallest matters? Know ye not that we shall judge angels? how much more things that pertain to this life? If then ye have judgments of things pertaining to this life, set them to judge who are least esteemed in the church. I speak to your shame. Is it so, that there is not a wise man among you? no, not one that shall be able to judge between his brethren? But brother goeth to law with brother, and that before the unbelievers. Now therefore there is utterly a fault among you, because ye go to law one with another. Why do ye not rather take wrong? why do ye not rather suffer yourselves to be defrauded? (1 Corinthians 6:1-7).

In recent years, the Seventh-day Adventist Church has begun to face a dilemma. More and more people are claiming to be Seventh-day Adventists who are not organizationally, by membership, attached to the Seventh-day Adventist denomination. This was not a common situation for Seventh-day Adventists in the past. There were breakaway movements, such as the Reformed Seventh-day Adventists, who separated under great provocation from apostate denominational leadership in Europe. Such breakaway movements were relatively scarce; now, however, there is a drift toward congregational philosophy, and the establishment of small groups who continue to call themselves Seventh-day Adventists while separating from membership in the Seventh-day Adventist denomination.

In some denominations, this would not be a serious problem. The Lutheran Church has a number of different fellowships, as the Baptist Church, the Church of God, and many other churches do. However, to the leaders of the Seventh-day Adventist Church, the use of the denominational name by those who had not sought their permission was intolerable. It was seen as presenting a threat to the good name of the Seventh-day Adventist Church, so it was decided that strong action should be taken. Many members were shocked when the name Seventh-day Adventist and its abbreviation, SDA, along with some other names very closely related to the Adventist Church, such as The Review and Herald, were registered as a trademark. This action was a leaning upon the arm of flesh rather than upon the arm of the Lord.

All faithful Seventh-day Adventist members deplore the fact that those not truly representative of our faith would adopt the name Seventh-day Adventist; nevertheless, that is an altogether different response than using the arm of the state to enforce the edicts of the denomination. The authors believe that the church leaders should write letters, urging such people to discontinue the use of the name Seventh-day Adventist. Though the results of such letters would be minimal, a statement would be on file pointing out the disapproval of the major body of the church to such groups.

The Seventh-day Adventist Church has now begun to witness another phenomenon. In some cases, faithful members are being driven out of the church. (This problem has continued to increase dramatically over the last few years.) Sometimes disfellowshipment is used. In other cases members are forced to leave because of the constant apostasy being taught from the pulpits and in Sabbath school classes. Some members decide that it is not wise to continue to worship in such an environment: especially is it so with those who have children growing up in the church. Still others are so startled by the Pentecostal drift in many of our local churches that they feel there is no way they can stay in a church which has chosen to introduce devices of Satan rather than following the God-given, inspiring service patterns that were appropriated in the Seventh-day Adventist Church in early years. Whatever the reasons, whether the separation be voluntary or involuntary, there is now a movement gaining great momentum, especially in the

Western world, for the establishment of little home churches, where those who are participating are able to worship in spirit and in truth. It is only natural that some of these churches have decided, whether they be faithful or unfaithful to the Advent faith, to retain the name Seventh-day Adventist.

Unquestionably, the legal action taken by the General Conference against a one-time unordained Seventh-day Adventist pastor, John Marik, has received the greatest notoriety. Here is a man little known, who, because of significant dreams he claims to have had, decided to sever himself from the Seventh-day Adventist Church and establish a little church of his own in a remote part of Hawaii. With approximately thirteen members, his church posed little or no threat to the church organization, but certain church leaders decided that this was to be a test case. Large numbers of Seventh-day Adventists were incensed when the lawsuit was filed against John Marik for the use of the name Seventh-day Adventist Congregational Church. It was, quite apparently, a David-and-Goliath struggle, and a complete rejection of the Bible injunction not to sue a brother.

Some asserted that John Marik was no longer a brother because he had withdrawn from the fellowship of the church, but that did not placate the uneasiness of many. Marik made a poor defense, and the district court ruled against him and in favor of the General Conference. Later, with the help of legal aid, John Marik appealed to the Federal Appeals Court in San Francisco, and the judges ruled that the case must be reheard. In the court's legal opinion, it was held that there may be a case made for the name Seventh-day Adventist being a generic name, that is, a name that describes a particular product or service. If the courts were to sustain such an opinion, it would be impossible to sue some individual or group under the trademark legislation.

Subsequently, John Marik's personal problems led him to an agreement with the General Conference in which he agreed to desist from the use of the name Seventh-day Adventist. Thus ended the case.

On two occasions, Colin met John Marik. John Marik came unannounced to visit him and talk with him for a couple of hours on one occasion when Colin was ministering in the Southern California Conference. Colin was unimpressed by the man and his story, but still strongly supported his right to freedom to practice religion as he saw fit. The second encounter was at a campmeeting in Southeastern California Conference territory, and again Colin's opinion of the authenticity of Marik's claim was unchanged.

Before the resolution of the John Marik case, the church decided to sue the Kinship SDA Association. This Kinship group is a group of practicing homosexuals and their supporters. They are apparently not interested in human, and more importantly, divine help to overcome their homosexual tendencies; rather, they seek to assert their right to participation in the church as practicing homosexuals and lesbians.

It is the authors' contention that those with homosexual tendencies, who, under the power of Christ, are gaining victory day by day, have every right to full participation and even leadership roles within the Seventh-day Adventist Church. However, homosexual practice is strongly condemned in the Word of God, and should not be tolerated. (See Romans 1:26,27, Leviticus 18:22, Leviticus 20:13, 1 Corinthians 6:9, and 1 Timothy 1:10.)

We believed that denominational leaders had every right to strongly urge that the Kinship group drop the SDA designation in their name, for it was inconsistent with the standards that God had established for His holy people. Still, we felt totally uncomfortable with the lawsuit that they filed. First and foremost, we were, on Biblical grounds, opposed to taking men and women to courts of law. Secondly, knowing full well the power of the homosexual lobby, we supposed that the chances of success in such a lawsuit would be small. So it proved. On October 3, 1991, Judge Mariana R. Pfaelzer ruled in favor of the Kinship group using the initials SDA and the name Seventh-day Adventist. The judge held that many of the Kinship members were members of the Seventh-day Adventist Church in "good and regular standing," so this was the religion of their identity. For this reason, the court upheld their right to use the name.

A side issue here is the tragedy that active, known homosexuals are still members of the Seventh-day Adventist Church. It surely is at this level that the good name of the church should be protected.

In response to the judge's decision, the leadership of the church placed a statement in the *Adventist Review* under the title "General Conference Will Not Appeal Trademark Decision." It read as follows,

> The General Conference will not appeal a Federal Court ruling that a homosexual support group may use the name "Seventh-day Adventist," reports Robert W. Nixon, associate of the Office of General Council of the General Conference.

Judge Mariana R. Pfaelzer of the U. S. District Court for Central California ruled that the support group, Kinship International, "is entitled to use the name 'Seventh-day Adventist'" to identify the religion of the group's membership.

The judge felt prelimited application of the decision to the homosexual group. "Arguably," she wrote, "use of the name 'Seventh-day Adventist' in conjunction with 'church' would require a different result."

The judge rejected arguments that an application of trademark laws would be a violation of religious liberty. "After reviewing the case authority [prior court decisions]," Judge Pfaelzer said, "It is clear that enjoining SDA Kinship from using the name 'Seventh-day Adventist' or 'SDA' would not prevent it from practicing the religion" (*Adventist Review*, November 14, 1991, p. 6).

There were those who were still deeply concerned by the judge's ruling. Perhaps those who would use the name "Seventh-day Adventist" and "church" together will still be threatened with a lawsuit, especially as the General Conference Committee, on October 31, voted "that it continue to protect the church and its members from misuses of the church's name" (Ibid.).

The United States is not the only nation in which Seventh-day Adventist church leaders are attempting to use the state to enforce the church's decisions. The leadership of the South Pacific Division sought an injunction from the High Court of the State of Victoria, Australia, to prevent the publication of *The Protestant*, a newspaper that puts forth the concepts expressed in *The Great Controversy* and Uriah Smith's book *Daniel and the Revelation*. The division lost the case and thousands of sacred dollars by pursuing this matter in defiance of the plain Word of God. *The Protestant* continues to be printed, the third edition being an issue of one million copies.

Our counsel to our leaders is to refrain from any further such action. These actions are destroying confidence in the leadership of the church for a significant number of faithful Seventh-day Adventists. The costs are too great, and the results too divisive. The God of heaven is well able to protect His church. Furthermore, Sister White warns us that the combination of the iron and miry clay represents the union of churchcraft and statecraft.

> The mingling of churchcraft and statecraft is represented by the iron and the clay. This union is weakening all the power of the churches. This investing the church with the power of the state will bring evil results. Men have almost passed the point of God's forbearance (SDA Bible Commentary Vol. 4 p.1168).

It was the union of church and state particularly which led to the worst abuses by the Roman Catholic Church. Our sin will be no smaller than theirs if we continue to pursue a course of using the state to enforce our ecclesiastical desires. It must stop if we are to be a church that truly upholds the concepts of religious liberty and the rights of those with whom we disagree. God has given His church leadership no authority to use the courts of the land to enforce their views, even when correct.

There is another matter that is a great burden to the authors. We believe that, frequently, leadership is identifying the wrong people as the ones who are responsible for the misuse and misrepresentation of the sacred, God-given name "Seventh-day Adventist." Many of our people today, including some leaders and pastors, are not representative of the message in either belief or practice. They are dishonoring the church by their teachings and lifestyles. Such people truly are bringing great impotency to the church. They are largely responsible for the terrible divisions that are occurring in the ranks of God's church today.

The faithful witnesses and warnings of earnest preachers and laymen are not the cause of division in the church today. Division comes from many areas, of which we will suggest a few:

1. The tragic events of 1956, when some leaders of our church denied some of the great pillars of our faith

2. The willful continuance in competitive sports in schools and colleges contrary to the counsel of the Lord (as well as against the decision of the Annual Council of 1989)

3. The dishonesty that has been revealed in such cases as the Davenport scandal

4. The collapse of Harris Pine Mills

5. The forty-million-dollar loss of Adventist Health Systems North

6. The supermarket scandal of the Lake Regional Conference

7. The P.U.C. Church tithe scandal

8. Trademark legislation

These have caused a decided lack of confidence in the financial integrity of those entrusted with leadership in the church; though most leaders are not involved in abuse of their positions, all tend to be branded by the sinful practices of the unconverted few.

Without doubt, the unfair attacks on self-supporting ministries have caused a marked loss of confidence in leadership on the part of many of the most faithful members of God's church. The time has come for us to put aside these degrading experiences of the past, come together in the truth and love of the gospel, and take up the challenge of the hour: to work together as men and brethren united in a truth that sanctifies. Then, and only then, can laity and ministry link hands, and together, under the power of the Latter Rain, take the message of salvation to every far-flung corner of this world.

16
Church Discipline—
A Growing Concern

A s the early church began to disintegrate, and the purity of the faith began to be diluted with pagan concepts, it was more difficult to call for unity built upon the truth that sanctifies. However, that was (and is) the only form of unity that the Bible upholds.

Sanctify them through thy truth: thy word is truth (John 17:17).

And for their sakes I sanctify myself, that they also might be sanctified through the truth (John 17:19).

And he gave some, apostles; and some, prophets; and some, evangelists; and some, pastors and teachers; for the perfecting of the saints, for the work of the ministry, for the edifying of the body of Christ: till we all come in the unity of the faith, and of the knowledge of the Son of God, unto a perfect man, unto the measure of the stature of the fullness of Christ: that we henceforth be no more children, tossed to and fro, and carried about with every wind of doctrine, by the sleight of men, and cunning craftiness, whereby they lie in wait to deceive; but speaking the truth in love, may grow up into him in all things, which is the head, even Christ (Ephesians 4:11-15).

Ellen White puts it this way,

There is no sanctification aside from the truth (*Fundamentals of Christian Education,* p. 432).

Unity is the sure result of Christian perfection (*Sanctified Life,* p. 85).

When truth is no longer the principle that unites God's people, and false doctrines and theories come into the church, disunity quickly becomes apparent. Instead of earnest appeals to return to the truth, it becomes popular to urge tolerance. Thus an eclectic or pluralistic belief system is developed with varied and often incompatible views, supposedly equally acceptable, within the church. Once we move away from the clear, unequivocal truth, we are certainly on Satan's territory, for we are substituting the doctrines of devils for the doctrines of Christ. It is ironic but understandable that usually the only belief system that seems intolerable under such circumstances is that of faithfulness to God's truth.

There is another issue that arises when truth no longer is the basis of church unity. Leaders and members alike are forced to look for another basis upon which to attempt to bring cohesion to the body of the church. Those who hold unwaveringly to the truth as the only basis of unity are perceived as arbitrary, intolerant, and divisive, and often become the subjects of the scorn, ridicule and persecution of those who are unfaithful.

There is a further development that irrevocably takes place when truth is no longer the basis of church fellowship. The moral, spiritual and behavioral tone of the members deteriorates markedly. This creates a great dilemma for the church, for if all those who have fallen away from truth and righteousness are disfellowshiped, there will be a mighty exodus from the church. Therefore, there is a tendency to overlook both doctrinal apostasy and sinful lifestyles. Whereas once the church would have dealt swiftly with adulterers, fornicators, thieves, and the like, now, through a false profession of love and concern, the most vile sins are covered under the cloak of "righteous" compassion. The church thus retains many members who are motivated by Satan, and who live a life in conformity to his deceptions. These people are used by Satan to become the persecutors of the righteous. Their votes in church board and business meetings are often used to discipline and disfellowship God's faithful people.

When truth and sanctification are no longer the standard by which church membership is evaluated, a new standard must be established. Inevitably, this new standard is built upon "loyalty to the church." In a not-too-subtle way, Satan makes that the basis upon which membership is retained. "Loyalty to the church" comes to be interpreted as "a non-critical attitude toward the church," "a non-critical attitude toward other members of the church," "a non-critical attitude toward the leaders and pastors of the church." The financial support of the church also becomes an issue.

In the Middle Ages, it is well-known that some of the most diabolical men became the favorites of the church by giving large donations to the church from the abundance of their wealth. Many years ago, while still in Australia, Colin was confronted by a similar situation. A member of the church Colin belonged to had not attended church regularly for many years. He was constantly breaking the Sabbath, and had wholly separated himself from the fellowship of the church, except for a possible visit once or twice a year for a special occasion. However, once each year he gave a sizable donation to the church. When the issue of his continued membership came before the church board, there was strong opposition to the idea of disfellowshiping him, because "he gives generously to the church every year." In reality, the man gave very little of the wealth he unquestionably had. Nevertheless, it seemed sufficient for some of the board members to feel that he had bought his right to retain his membership in the church. Surely such an approach is totally unacceptable to God.

The authors believe that the Spirit of Prophecy emphasizes only two reasons for separating members from the church— unrighteousness and/or doctrinal apostasy. When men or women move away from the clear pillars of the Seventh-day Adventist faith, they must be disfellowshiped from the body of believers if prayerful and genuinely loving efforts to restore them fail to change their beliefs. The same is true in terms of a life of sin. It is important that in loving concern we seek out these apostatized members and try to woo them back through the principles of Christian love, but if they continue in their ways of wickedness, the church has a moral obligation to disfellowship them. Otherwise, the glory of the Lord departs from the church, and it becomes impotent and ineffective in the mission to which it is called.

Many churches who have members in deep apostasy or open sin do not address the issue. They retain membership, God is dishonored, and the church is impotent. It is an even greater abomination when such acts are performed by the minister of a church, but proper disciplinary action is not always applied. For example, Colin knows of two cases of ministers in the United States who have been found guilty of dishonesty in the civil courts of the land, yet who are continuing in their ministry. It is hard to believe that this could be allowed. It is well-known that there are situations where ministers have been guilty of adultery, and yet have continued in their ministry. One does not have to ask the question, Is God honored?

Now we address how this has affected the *Church Manual* and the procedures of discipline in the church. In the 1932 *Church Manual* there are four grounds for disfellowshiping. In the 1990 *Church Manual* there are eleven grounds for disfellowshiping. We hasten to add that quite a number of the additional ones are really subdivisions of those that were in the 1932 *Manual*. However, in a tragic decision at the General Conference Session in Dallas in 1980, another reason for disfellowshiping was added to the already-too-long list. It passed with barely a ruffle, yet intuitively we knew that this was going to be the basis upon which faithful members of the church would be cast out.

It is important to note that this additional ground for disfellowshipment was added 136 years after the Great Disappointment, and 117 years after the formation of the General Conference. For all of that period of time, this reason for disfellowshiping was never used or needed. This new ground for disfellowshiping added in 1980 is now number seven on page 160 of the 1990 *Church Manual*. It reads, "Adhering to or taking part in a divisive or disloyal movement or organization." It will be noticed that this allows for an extraordinarily subjective evaluation for disfellowshipment. Theft, adultery, or doctrinal deviation are objective criteria for disfellowshipment; but this ground calls for the human analysis of whether someone has been disloyal or divisive. We are filled with great alarm, because throughout the ages, God's faithful people have been referred to as dividers of the church. Elijah is a classic example. When met by King Ahab, the king asked, "Art thou he that troubleth Israel?" (1 Kings 18:7.) Of course, it was not Elijah who troubled Israel; it was the apostasy and idolatry of Ahab. The prophet made this fact clear in his response.

> And he answered, I have not troubled Israel; but thou, and thy father's house, in that ye have forsaken the commandments of the LORD, and thou hast followed Baalim (1 Kings 18:18).

Surely the reason for trouble in ancient Israel is identical with the reason for the division in the church today. We are forsaking the commandments of God and following the paths of paganism. There are only two systems of worship in the world: true Christian worship and pagan worship. Like Israel of old, there is today much evidence of pagan practices within the Seventh-day Adventist Church. (See C. D. Standish, R. R. Standish, *Spiritism In the Seventh-day Adventist Church,* Hartland Publications.) The faithful members of the church who want to stand by the old paths, wherein is the good way, are coming under tremendous pressure. Cries are being heard, calling for unity in diversity, but these are just the echo of the World Council of Churches and the ecumenical movement. They are wholly inappropriate for the remnant church of God. There can be no unity in diversity. It is a contradiction of terms that has no valid meaning. Unity comes in truth, not in diversity, and truth is unadulterated and untrammeled by human wisdom or philosophy.

Today, as we predicted in 1980, the seventh of the grounds for disfellowshiping is increasingly becoming the chief reason for disfellowshiping. Godless men and women living a life of sin and deception are allowed to retain their membership in God's church, while faithful men and women are thrust out. Indeed, the Roman Catholic idea of excommunication seems to be more accurate in the case of Elder and Mrs. Graham Cabbin (see chapter seventeen), for they were told that they would not even be welcome to worship in the church. Why? In the letter sent to them, dated July 8, 1991, they were informed, "Reason for action: Church Manual, page 160 (number seven), adhering to/taking part in a divisive/disloyal movement."

Even more recently, Garry Romano (who gave up a career as a commercial airline captain to become a Seventh-day Adventist) and Vada Kum Yuen (daughter of a lifelong missionary to a South Sea island) were disfellowshiped. When the Cairns Church of the North Australia Conference overwhelmingly voted not to disfellowship these faithful Adventists, the North Australia Conference leadership went to the extraordinary length of having the members disband their own church so the conference could circumvent the decision of the local church and disfellowship these loyal Seventh-day Adventists.

The authors know faithful people in Great Britain, Switzerland, Yugoslavia, Hungary, Poland, Germany, Canada, the United States, Australia and New Zealand who have been confronted by this particular 1980 addition to the grounds for disfellowshipment.

How sad is the result when we take one step away from the Lord! However, we should not be surprised that it is taking place. The warnings of Scripture are clear.

Woe be unto the pastors that destroy and scatter the sheep of my pasture! saith the LORD. Therefore thus saith the LORD God of Israel against the pastors that feed my people; Ye have scattered my flock, and driven them away, and have not visited them: behold, I will visit upon you the evil of your doings, saith the LORD (Jeremiah 23:1, 2).

Son of man, prophesy against the shepherds of Israel, prophesy, and say unto them, Thus saith the Lord GOD unto the shepherds; Woe be to the shepherds of Israel that do feed themselves! should not the shepherds feed the flocks? (Ezekiel 34:2).

My people hath been lost sheep: their shepherds have caused them to go astray, they have turned them away on the mountains: they have gone from mountain to hill, they have forgotten their restingplace (Jeremiah 50:6).

Beware of false prophets, which come to you in sheep's clothing, but inwardly they are ravening wolves (Matthew 7:15).

Paul also said,

For I know this, that after my departing shall grievous wolves enter in among you, not sparing the flock (Acts 20:29).

However, the Lord gives hope for those who have been driven out.

And I will restore thy judges as at the first, and thy counsellors as at the beginning: afterward thou shalt be called, The city of righteousness, the faithful city. Zion shall be redeemed with judgment, and her converts with righteousness (Isaiah 1:26, 27).

And I will gather the remnant of my flock out of all countries whither I have driven them, and will bring them again to their folds; and they shall be fruitful and increase. And I will set up shepherds over them which shall feed them: and they shall fear no more, nor be dismayed, neither shall they be lacking, saith the LORD (Jeremiah 23:3, 4).

And I will set up one shepherd over them, and he shall feed them, even my servant David; he shall feed them, and he shall be their shepherd. And I the LORD will be their God, and my servant David a prince among them; I the LORD have spoken it (Ezekiel 34:23, 24).

I will gather them that are sorrowful for the solemn assembly, who are of thee, to whom the reproach of it was a burden. Behold, at that time I will undo all that afflict thee: and I will save her that halteth, and gather her that was driven out; and I will get them praise and fame in every land where they have been put to shame. At that time will I bring you again, even in the time that I gather you: for I will make you a name and a praise among all people of the earth, when I turn back your captivity before your eyes, saith the LORD (Zephaniah 3:18-20).

God has made promises to His people: if they are faithful, He will not desert them, and ultimately He will redress the wickedness of those unfaithful servants who have driven them out. There is no reason to be discouraged or downhearted, for the Lord is our strength.

17
Disfellowshipment

At the 1980 General Conference Session in Dallas, Texas, the delegates made two very serious decisions. One caused a great furor at the session: the adoption of the 27 Statements of Fundamental Beliefs. Later we will explore the tragic results of the decision to vote in these twenty-seven statements of belief, and the role it has played in the drift toward credalism.

A second decision that attracted much less attention, but which has proved to be just as disastrous to the church, was the adoption of a new basis for church discipline and disfellowshiping. It now appears as item number seven in the *Church Manual*. It reads as follows:

7. Adhering to or taking part in a divisive or disloyal movement or organization (*Church Manual*, 1991 Edition, p. 160).

Russell was a delegate to the 1980 General Conference Session, and though not a delegate, Colin was in attendance. Intuitively they knew that this new ground for disfellowshiping would lead to the persecution of faithful, truth-believing members of the church. So it is proving to be with rapidly increasing momentum.

From the time of the Great Disappointment, 136 years had passed without the need of such a ground for disfellowshiping, and since the organization of the General Conference in 1863, 117 years had passed by without this ground being a basis for disfellowshipment. The adding of this new requirement should have caused great alertness on the part of the delegates at the General Conference Session, but it did not; it passed with hardly a flutter.

There are only two grounds for disfellowshipment validated by inspiration: 1) doctrinal apostasy, and 2) living a life of open sin, violating the commandments of God.

Even a casual review of this new ground for disfellowshipment indicates the subjectivity that it involves. Someone has to determine what is "divisive" and what is a "disloyal movement or organization." It is usual today to make this interpretation in terms of those who are standing for truth against the widespread apostasy, worldliness, and sin within the church. Thus, individuals who are the strongest supporters of God, His truth, and His righteousness are the most vulnerable to being disfellowshiped on these grounds.

There is no question that the church has a right—a God-given responsibility—to disfellowship those who are unfit representatives of our message. The servant of the Lord said that there would be those who have sinned so grievously that if they are ever going to get to heaven they will have to do it outside of the church. Their lives have been such a disgrace to the cause of God that, though they may later repent, the character of their influence has been such that it would be unwise to accept them back into church fellowship.

Frequently, Sister White has associated the apostasy and worldliness in the church with the sin of Achan. Achan pretended to have fellowship with the people of God, while he coveted the world. This brought not only impotency to Israel, but also great destruction. In today's church, members are behaving and living after the practices of the world, and misrepresenting the pure and holy gospel that God has given to the church. This brings feebleness to the work of the church in its efforts to bring souls into the kingdom of heaven.

Because apostasy and worldliness is so prevalent in the church, it is not surprising that there is today such a dearth of true spirituality and such an impotency in bringing the glorious three angels' messages to the world. Sister White issued repeated warnings concerning this:

> If the presence of one Achan was sufficient to weaken the whole camp of Israel, can we be surprised at the little success which attends our efforts when every church and almost every family has its Achan? (*Testimonies for the Church,* Volume 5, page 157).

> I saw that the Israel of God must arise and renew their strength in God by renewing and keeping their covenant with Him. Covetousness, selfishness, love of money, and love of the world, are all through the ranks of Sabbathkeepers. These evils are destroying the spirit of sacrifice among God's people. Those that have this covetousness in their hearts are not aware of it.

It has gained upon them imperceptibly, and unless it is rooted out, their destruction will be as sure as was Achan's (*Testimonies for the Church*, Volume 1, page 140).

No man lives to himself. Shame, defeat, and death were brought upon Israel by one man's sin. That protection which had covered their heads in the time of battle was withdrawn. Various sins that are cherished and practiced by professed Christians bring the frown of God upon the church (*Testimonies for the Church*, Volume 4, page 493).

There is now an alarming trend worldwide. Those who are steeped in sin are being retained on the church record books as members in good and regular standing, on the basis that we must show them love and concern, while others are ruthlessly disfellowshiped for expressing their deep concern for the apostasy and worldliness in the church. These people, in their love for God and for the church, try to awake their Laodicean brethren, but in the process those who resist their earnest pleadings turn upon them and declare that they are the troublers of Israel. They are called critics, legalists, and perfectionists, names which wholly misrepresent these sincere and godly people. Often such members are urged to desist their call to God's people for repentance and reformation, and are expelled from the church of God for their faithful testimonies. When Colin was in Europe in the summer of 1991, he found such disfellowshiped people in Great Britain, Germany, Switzerland, Yugoslavia, Hungary, Poland, and the former Soviet Union. It is not necessary to repeat the story of the mass disfellowshipment that took place many years ago in Hungary when the president of a union illegally disfellowshiped hundreds of faithful Adventists who were fighting against his ecumenical and apostate trend. We will give a few other examples.

In Poland, Colin met Brother Tadeusz Fojcik. Tadeusz had a great desire to translate the 1888 materials on righteousness by faith by Jones and Waggoner into the Polish language. He was warned to cease, as this was not the work of laity, but of the denomination. However, when he recognized that some of the Spirit of Prophecy books were being translated inaccurately, especially in the area of righteousness by faith, victory over sin, and perfection of character, and commenced to redress this apparently deliberate effort to water down the great three angels' messages, he was forthwith disfellowshiped. Colin was greatly moved when, the morning after arriving at Tadeusz's home, he saw Tadeusz's 91-year-old father putting on his helmet and getting onto a motorbike with a little side car to go out to do his missionary work. This is the kind of dedicated person that is being held in question today in God's church.

Colin was also moved when, in Berlin, he stayed with Dr. Bernd Korinth. The Korinth family had lived in East Germany, and had spent many years faithfully resisting the communist efforts to destroy Christianity. Theirs had not been an easy task. Bernd's father was an ordained minister of the Seventh-day Adventist Church during this crisis. However, in the early 1980s, before the dismantling of communism, his family was brought over to West Berlin when the West Berlin government paid 80,000 marks to the East German government.

Dr. Korinth, an ear, nose and throat specialist, and some of the other members of his family were vigorous in their mission outreach. They formed the Berlin Missionary Society, and enthusiastically gave testimony of the Lord's leading in their work. Soon they were asked not to relate any experiences associated with the Berlin Missionary Society in testimony meetings. Bernd began a one-half-hour radio program on a Berlin radio station. He spoke for approximately one-quarter of an hour, and invited his retired pastor father to answer called-in questions from the listening audience. When told by the conference that they must cease this outreach, they chose to follow the higher calling of Christ.

When they refused to discontinue the broadcasts, they were disfellowshiped. Even Pastor Korinth, at 83 years of age, and after 55 years as an ordained minister in the work of God, often under the most difficult circumstances in East Berlin, was disfellowshiped, and his ordination was revoked. The family had thought that they had come out of bondage into freedom when they had come to West Berlin, but indeed they faced a greater bondage in God's church that has been extraordinarily hard for them to handle.

When I met Pastor Korinth, he was 86 years old. Nevertheless, to the best of his strength, he was continuing in faithful witnessing efforts. Such disgraceful disfellowshiping must be a source of great sorrow to God.

The work of disfellowshiping faithful people in England is expanding. It started with Margaret Murray, a dedicated member of the Eastbourne Church in southern England. It moved on to Norwich. There, a number of very faithful Adventists were seeking to help their fellow-members understand the call for accepting truth and righteousness that Christ is making to this end-time generation. (Norwich is a large city in East Anglia, but our membership there is very small.) A group of ten or twelve people formed the nucleus of those earnestly burdened for their fellow church members. However, in July of 1991, efforts were made to disfellowship these people, and indeed, Brother and Sister Graham Cabbin were disfellowshiped. Brother and Sister Cabbin have been Seventh-day Adventists for well over 50 years, and now, in their eighth decade of life, they were disfellowshiped. In effect, they were actually excommunicated, for they were also asked not to attend the church. Brother Cabbin is a former elder of the Norwich Church and a former elder of the largest church in the North British Conference, the Camp Hill Church, in Birmingham, England. This man has brought many men and women to the Seventh-day Adventist Church; he had at the time three souls ready for baptism, but the pastor refused to baptize them because of their attendance at the Gazeley Fellowship meetings.

The Gazeley meetings are held approximately six times a year, and men and women from various parts of Britain come together for a weekend retreat to hear speakers presenting the fullness of the Advent message, the three angels' messages. These meetings had their origin in Witley, in February 1985, and were first held in Gazeley in June of 1986, when a team of Hartland speakers made presentations at the old Anglican rectory in that village. Many hundreds of faithful people have been blessed by the ministry there, and a significant number have been led to a clearer understanding of the Advent message, and have made their own personal commitment to God and to His truth.

Not only were Brother and Sister Cabbin disfellowshiped, but their three baptismal candidates, who were in regular attendance but had been refused the rite of baptism, were also told that they were no longer welcome to worship in the church. In his letter, the pastor said that he hoped this would lead to unity in the church and to the opportunity to bring others into the church. Of course, such has not been and will not be the result of turning away the most dedicated soul-winners in the church. This little group has been forced to worship in a dental clinic belonging to one of the other faithful members, Sister Jean Rose. They average about fifteen in attendance, and are still on fire for the Lord.

Others who have been greatly blessed and have been leaders in the Gazeley Fellowship have been denied membership in the newly-formed Bury-St. Edmunds Church. These include Richard Humphries, who is the organizer of the Gazeley Fellowship, and Roy Vesey, both of whom are dedicated, faithful, loyal Seventh-day Adventists.

There has also been disfellowshiping at the Portsmouth Church in southern England.

Of course, these actions are not limited to Europe; we see them in Canada, the United States, New Zealand, Australia, and no doubt other parts of the world. However, they are especially prevalent in the Western world. Surely the Lord is calling us to uphold the faithful and to remove the apostates and the worldlings from the midst of God's people. However, even this latter work must be done only after prayerful and earnest dialogue with and encouragement and entreaties to the ones who have fallen. Some, no doubt, will be restored, but others will, with great regret, have to be removed so that the church will be able to move forward in the power of the everlasting gospel.

18

The Ordination of Women

Throughout the Word of God are numerous examples of women playing mighty roles in the work of God. Women such as Miriam, Deborah, Huldah, Ruth, Esther, the various Marys, Martha, Dorcas and Lydia illustrate this fact. However, during the whole course of biblical history, not one woman was ordained to the priesthood of God's church. Today, in the spotlight of the women's liberation movement, the thrust of many churches has been for the ordination of women. Many mainline Protestant churches have authorized and even encouraged the ordination of women, although in most cases this decision did not come without a titanic struggle. Now the Seventh-day Adventist Church faces the same pressure. What is the proper role that God has given for women in His church? That is the issue.

The arguments for ordination of women are very fragile. Some suggest that because there is no direct injunction against the ordination of women in the Bible, it should not be forbidden. Others have urged that the ordination of women would have been wrong sociologically in the times of the Bible, but now, with a different sociological situation, the ordination of women would be wholly appropriate. Let us examine the facts.

The argument that our sociological situation has changed the standard becomes quite tenuous when it is recognized that the Egyptians freely had priests and priestesses when the Israelites were in captivity. The various nations of the Canaanites whose territory Israel eventually inhabited all had priests and priestesses. This was (and is) the pattern of the pagans; yet, significantly, in spite of it being the custom of the day, the Israelites were never permitted by God to appoint priestesses. The appointing of priestesses along with priests is part of pagan symbolism, not of Christianity, and the Lord would not allow such.

To see this issue in its true light, we must understand that paganism is established upon the idea of balancing the cosmic forces in the universe. This false religious practice calls for "balancing" the polar opposites such as good and bad, height and depth, light and darkness, hot and cold, and male and female.

It is not surprising that the pagans had good gods and bad gods, as they had male gods and female gods, and that they related to them though male priests and female priests. This concept was central to pagan worship, but it was foreign to God's people. In God's system, priests alone were ordained. From time to time, women were chosen as prophetesses, but never as priests or leaders in the synagogues or in God's church. That principle God has maintained for almost six thousand years. It is inconceivable that He would spontaneously alter this principle in these last days. It must be recognized that this issue is not a sociological issue: it is an issue that divides between Christian worship on one hand and pagan worship on the other.

The women's liberation movement has been the chief catalyst in causing the sociological situation to change. God did not ordain this movement. Indeed, God spoke very strongly against it. In the 1860s there was a similar women's rights movement, and God, through His servant, strongly condemned it:

> Those who feel called out to join the movement in favor of woman's rights and the so-called dress reform might as well sever all connection with the third angel's message. The spirit which attends the one cannot be in harmony with the other (*Testimonies for the Church,* Volume 1, p. 457).

It is unthinkable that what comes out of the godless women's liberation movement can be of value to Seventh-day Adventists. It is wholly unacceptable to God and to man. Christian women must recognize that in motherhood they have a role greater than any minister, and the equality of men and women that we speak of is an equality in diversity.

> There is a God above, and the light and glory from His throne rests upon the faithful mother as she tries to educate her children to resist the influence of evil. No other work can equal hers in importance. She has not, like the artist, to paint a form of beauty upon canvas, nor, like the sculptor, to chisel it from marble. She has not, like the author, to embody a noble thought in words of power, nor, like the musician, to express a beautiful sentiment in melody. It is hers, with the help of God, to develop in a human soul the likeness of the divine (*The Ministry of Healing,* pp. 377-378).

Unfortunately, many mothers have abdicated this God-given privilege, just as many fathers have abdicated their responsibility.

> As the priest of the household, he is accountable to God for the influence that he exerts over every member of the family (*Counsels to Parents, Teachers and Students,* p. 128).

That the issue of the ordination of women should become such a major problem in the Seventh-day Adventist Church is a sign that we are more and more influenced by the pressures of our environment. Frequently, the sociological conflicts of the day affect the Seventh-day Adventist Church, and ever since the 1960s, there has been an increasing pressure for what is called "sex equality."

Many years ago Colin read an article in the *Reader's Digest* by a woman physician which was entitled, "Equal But Different." The author pointed out, in a very splendid way, that equality did not mean sameness, and that it was important to recognize that the equality of the roles of women and men could never mean that they fulfill the same roles. Men and women were ordained to complement each other, not to be clones of each other. After sin entered the world, God made the matter of the relationship clear.

> Unto the woman he said, I will greatly multiply thy sorrow and thy conception; in sorrow thou shalt bring forth children; and thy desire shall be to thy husband, and he shall rule over thee (Genesis 3:16).

Throughout the Bible the leadership role of the husband or the male is confirmed.

> Wives, submit yourselves unto your own husbands, as unto the Lord. For the husband is the head of the wife, even as Christ is the head of the church (Ephesians 5:22, 23).

However, this does not mean that the wife must be subservient to every wish of the husband, for sometimes that might conflict with her duty to God. Paul clarifies this,

> Wives, submit yourselves unto your own husbands, as it is fit in the Lord (Colossians 3:18).

This principle pertains across the spectrum of male/female relationships. It is not the role of the husband to lord over the wife, to dominate her or to crush her individuality; it is his responsibility to be the patriarch, the priest, and the spiritual leader of the home. Men are likewise to be the leaders within the environment of the church congregation.

Western society today faces two phenomena. One is the abdication of the responsibility of leadership by many men, and the other is the drive of many women to take the role that God has ordained for men alone. Each seems to feed the other. God is calling for Christians to re-establish the true roles of men and women as models for the next generation of young people.

It is evident that both males and females have a critical role to play in the finishing of God's work. Indeed, the servant of the Lord has placed the role of a mother ahead of that of any other human being, including the minister. While this will not be understood by most men and women of the world, it should be clearly understood by all Seventh-day Adventists.

In 1975, Colin was a member of a General Conference ad hoc committee that was addressing issues to be presented to the General Conference Quinquennial Session due to be held in July of that year in Vienna, Austria. Sub-committees were set up to review various issues. He was stunned when the General Conference Vice-President chairing the committee asked him to chair the sub-committee on the ordination of women. Colin pleaded for mercy, but the Vice-President insisted. When the group of ten or twelve met, Colin pointed out that the only valid approach was to search the Scriptures and Spirit of Prophecy to determine the plan of the Lord. To this the sub-committee readily agreed. Being at the General Conference headquarters, they had at their disposal the resources of the White Estate. When the sub-committee reassembled, the members reported no Biblical evidence for women's ordination as elders or pastors, but much evidence for their active participation in the spiritual mission of the church. From the Spirit of Prophecy only one statement was found that the sub-committee members felt they must address.

> Women who are willing to consecrate some of their time to the service of the Lord should be appointed to visit the sick, looking after the young, and ministering to the necessities of the poor. They should be set apart for this work by prayer and laying on of hands (*The Review and Herald,* July 9, 1895).

However, the sub-committee noticed that this was a part-time service, and that in the context of the article it certainly was not dealing with the work of a minister or elder. While the passage in no way referred to ordination, for frequently the laying on of hands is not associated with ordination (e.g. the laying on of hands for the sick), the sub-committee recommended to the full committee that further study be given to the possibility of the ordination of women to the office of deaconess. The sub-committee reported that there was no divine counsel to support the ordination of women elders nor women pastors.

The report was very poorly received, and two now-retired General Conference leaders expressed their adamant belief that we must move toward the ordination of women elders. Colin was shocked that all but one of the sub-committee members, in addition to himself, surrendered their "convictions" under this pressure and voted with the other members of the large committee to recommend that further consideration be given to moving toward the ordination of female local church elders. Though the measure was not implemented at that time, the die was cast, and it was just a matter of time. Today, hundreds of women have been ordained as local elders, and we can expect more such ordinations to take place in the future.

The authors are convinced that it is only a matter of time before full ordination of women to the gospel ministry will take place. In fact, the first meeting concerning the possible ordination of women took place in 1973. This is a sad example of the way God's people too often respond to sociological pressure rather than to the explicit Word of God. Since 1973 there have been many challenges and many conferences. There is no question that the push toward the ordination of women will succeed unless a miracle takes place.

Those who were in attendance at the 1990 General Conference Session witnessed the staggering battle that took place over the ordination of women pastors. Many were relieved when, by a solid majority, the ordination of women pastors was rejected. However, the very next day, under enormous pressure from North America, many of the overseas delegates weakened, and by a significant margin it was voted to allow women pastors to perform almost all the duties of an ordained minister of the church.

We predict that soon the ultimate goal will be achieved, allowing the ordination of women ministers. Some conferences, e.g. the Southeastern California Conference in 1991, came close to defying the General Conference rejection of the ordination of women. The struggles and determination that underscore this move for the ordination of women in the absence in inspiration of any evidence that God's approval is met was presented courageously by Laurel Damsteegt, a member of one of the study committees. Her statements are striking.

> Aside from the morning devotions and ensuing prayers, the group did not spend time praying. Neither did we spend time searching the Scriptures . . . we had not even attempted to come to the bottom of the Scriptural injunctions. . . . Behind the scenes someone had composed a statement that was pressed upon us as our only hope for accomplishing anything during this Commission.

> The proposal was a compromise; I doubt anyone was too happy about it. To please those who don't believe women should be ordained to the gospel ministry, it recommended that women should not be so ordained. To please those who want women to function as ministers, ordained or not, it recommended that they could function fully as ministers without being ordained.

> Suddenly it seemed that we were in a terrible rush to be done. We were divided into small groups, each with a General Conference administrator in charge, and given only thirty minutes to discuss the proposal's ramifications. And we were so much as told that the proposal could not be altered, or its parts voted on as separate components. It either flew as a whole package or our time at Cohutta was in vain. And really, there was no time to think it through (Laurel Damsteegt, *Adventists Affirm*, Fall 1989, pp. 44, 45).

In 1988, Colin was overnighting in Vancouver, British Columbia. The following morning he browsed through the newspaper placed at his motel door. The article that took his attention was written by a former moderator of the United Church of Canada. The issue was the desperate struggle in that church for the ordination of lesbian and homosexual ministers. Obviously, years before, the battle of women's ordination had been won, and now the battle had moved a step further in the thrust of the rights movement. Indeed, the article indicated that a special task force had actually recommended the careful evaluation of some homosexuals and lesbians for ordination. Colin was so moved by what he read, that he wrote an earnest letter to Elder Neal Wilson, then the General Conference President. In part, that letter said,

> I am not a prophet, but as a student of history I can predict that should the battle for the ordination of women be won in the Adventist Church, the next battle will be over the ordination of the homosexual and lesbian ministers. You may say, "impossible": I say, "inevitable." If we look at the trends in our church we can see how they follow, almost without fail, the trends in other churches. We just follow them 20 years behind. I am praying that God will overrule in this matter. We have to draw the line somewhere. I believe it is not good enough to allow us to go part-way down the hill. All the theological jargon and all the sociological argumentation cannot produce a "thus saith the Lord" to go ahead in the direction that we seem to be moving on the ordination of women (letter to Elder Neal C. Wilson).

The proponents of women's ordination are so determined that some protagonists have set up a special account whereby the tithe, and possibly the offerings of those supportive of the ordination of women can be placed, no doubt as a means of placing inordinate pressure upon the church. One thing is certain, the issue will surface again at the 1995 General Conference Session. With the use of placards, some proponents of the ordination of women have already marched in demonstration at an Annual Council.

The Seventh-day Adventist Church is built upon the Bible and the Bible only as the basis of faith and practice. To use any other basis is to follow the ways of Satan. The women's liberation movement is not of God, and is destined to lead its proponents away from the true principles that God has ordained. As Seventh-day Adventists we must exert every God-approved effort to fight yet another intrusion of Satan into our beloved church.

19

The Path of Controversy

I t is not our desire to add any more fuel to the explosive fires of controversy surrounding the tithe issue. Indeed, we believe wholeheartedly that the counsel of the servant of the Lord on this matter is wise and inspired. In what now has become a famous letter, Sister White, on January 22, 1905, wrote to Elder Watson, then the president of the Colorado Conference,

> The least you have to speak about the tithe that has been appropriated to the most needy and the most discouraging field in the world, the more sensible you will be.

This seems to us to be important counsel for today; it is certainly not our burden to incite angry debate. Colin has on at least two occasions urged leadership to refrain from keeping this issue alive. It is our considered opinion that the more that is said about the tithe issue in respect to where tithe is sent, the more likely it is that less will be sent to "regular" conference channels, and more will go into "irregular" channels.

Unsubstantiated and erroneous statements are being made by some denominational leaders against self-supporting leaders in efforts to discourage church members from returning tithe to self-supporting institutions. That is doing nothing to solve the dilemma of the church or to reduce the amount of tithe being sent to these institutions. The real dilemma is that (if reports are accurate) only about twenty-seven percent of all families in North America are returning a regular tithe to the denominational channels. We all need to work together to increase the awareness of our church members to their responsibility to return a faithful tithe to the Lord for the furtherance of His work.

One of the most unfortunate statements made in recent times was presented in a special supplement to the *Southwestern Union Record* by its president. (In this article, entitled "A Union President Shares His Views About Sending Tithe to Independent Ministries," many inflammatory statements were made about independent ministries that were neither justified nor profitable, and only added to the fires of controversy and division raging in our church.

However, that is not the burden of this chapter. We are here discussing what was said concerning tithe.) In answering the question, "How much tithe do *private organizations* receive each year?", he replied,

> Enough for the General Conference to cut back its home and overseas projects eight million dollars this year and call home some missionaries (*Southwestern Union Record* Supplement, January 1992 S-1).

What an unfounded statement! First, it is implied that there was no increase and probably a decrease in tithe in North America during 1991. In reality, the report from the General Conference leaders stated that there was a four percent increase in tithe in 1991, which was encouraging, considering the deep recession that the United States and Canada were then encountering.

Second, it is implied that the self-supporting ministries had enjoyed an increase of eight million dollars in tithe donations during 1991 over what they received in 1990. Not even in their wildest dreams could anyone imagine such an increase; indeed, it would be unreasonable to assume that anything like eight million dollars total was received in tithe by self-supporting ministries in any particular calendar year. In any case, no one knows—beside the Lord Himself—how much tithe has come into the treasuries of self-supporting institutions, especially since there are those who do not openly accept tithe, who tell their supporters that they do not accept checks marked "tithe." (This, of course, means that anyone may send tithe money if it is not directly marked as tithe.) Even taking all of this into account, it is highly improbable that eight million dollars of tithe is given to self-supporting institutions annually.

Third, there appears to be an increasing number of Seventh-day Adventists who are choosing to send tithe directly to mission fields, where they feel it has a much greater impact on the proclamation of the gospel and the forwarding of the work of God.

Fourth, the home fields are apparently using a greater percentage of the tithe than in former years, rather than passing it through the channels to the General Conference to be distributed to the overseas divisions. During the year prior to the 1990 General Conference Session, there were strong pressures from the local conferences to retain a higher percentage of the tithe than conferences had heretofore done. This was a measure received with some clear support from the then-president of the General Conference, Elder Neal Wilson, who spent time prior to the 1990 General Conference seeking ways to retain the same flow of appropriations to the mission field, should such a situation occur. In reality, it was hoped that at least some support would come directly out of the operating budget for the General Conference by downsizing the number of workers. There is no question that the current General Conference president, Elder Robert Folkenberg, is also seeking ways to reduce the General Conference staff and other administrative units in the church. We see this move as appropriate. We feel much less confidence in the idea of the local conferences retaining a higher share of the tithe income.

The tithe problems revolve around a wide number of issues. We recommend a number of publications for study. Perhaps the first and foremost would be the book *All About Tithe*, edited by Dr. Vernon Sparks. This book gives every statement in the Bible and Spirit of Prophecy concerning the tithe question. Every faithful Seventh-day Adventist should study this book. *A Fresh Look at the Storehouse*, by Dr. Lloyd and Leola Rosenvold, is also very helpful. Colin has prepared a most informative tract, entitled *Tithes and Offerings—A Biblical Perspective*, which is available from Hartland Publications.*

The situation concerning the tithe has certainly been heightened during the first part of the 1990s by a number of publications. Dr. Ralph Larson's article in the September 1991 issue of the magazine *Our Firm Foundation* has been strongly assailed by those believing that the denomination is the only storehouse or treasury of God. On the other hand, some have been just as incensed by the special supplement on tithe by Dr. Roger W. Coon, Associate Secretary of the Ellen G. White Estate, which appeared with the November 1991 issue of the *Adventist Review*.

We believe the best approach is to examine the main Spirit of Prophecy statements that cause misunderstanding and disagreements. We will leave it to the reader to make a decision what his

---

* These tracts are also available in quantity lots.

obligation and responsibility is under God. It is not our purpose to make the decision for any man or woman as to how to apply God's tithe. Each of us must stand responsible in the judgment for the way we decide to return our tithe, or perhaps more importantly, to where we return that tithe.

The following are some of the arguments and Spirit of Prophecy bases used by those who believe that tithe must be returned only through denominational channels. We also include some of the answers that have been used in response.

Argument One. God approves only of tithe being returned to the treasury of the conference (through the local church).

> Some have been dissatisfied and have said: "I will not longer pay my tithe; for I have no confidence in the way things are managed at the heart of the work." But will you rob God because you think the management of the work is not right? Make your complaint, plainly and openly, in the right spirit, to the proper ones. Send in your petitions for things to be adjusted and set in order; but do not withdraw from the work of God, and prove unfaithful, because others are not doing right (*Testimonies for the Church*, Volume 9, p. 249).

Response. Sister White is not here talking about the support of apostate ministers. She is talking about the fact that the management of the work is not what it ought to be. When it comes to apostasy, it is argued that Sister White has an entirely different answer.

> There are fearful woes for those who preach the truth, but are not sanctified by it, and also for those who consent to receive and maintain the unsanctified to minister to them in word and doctrine (*Testimonies for the Church*, Volume 1, pp. 261, 262).

> As there are woes for those who preach the truth while they are unsanctified in heart and life, so there are woes for those who receive and maintain the unsanctified in the position which they cannot fill (*Testimonies for the Church*, Volume 2, p. 552).

There is also clear evidence that the treasury is not limited to denominational sources. Statements such as,

I have myself appropriated my tithe to the most needy cases brought to my notice. I have been instructed to do this; and as the money is not withheld from the Lord's treasury, it is not a matter that should be commented upon, but it will necessitate my making known these matters, which I do not desire to do, because it is not best (Letter to Elder Watson, January 22, 1905).

Argument Two. There are fearful woes upon those who withhold the tithe from the church's treasury.

You who have been withholding your means from the cause of God, read the book of Malachi, and see what is spoken there in regard to tithes and offerings. Cannot you see that it is not best under any circumstances to withhold your tithes and offerings because you are not in harmony with everything your brethren do? The tithes and offerings are not the property of any man, but are to be used in doing a certain work for God. Unworthy ministers may receive some of the means thus raised; but dare anyone, because of this, withhold from the treasury, and brave the curse of God? I dare not. I pay my tithes gladly and freely (*Special Testimonies*, series A, number 1, page 27).

Response. Sister White is not here talking about sending tithe to self-supporting institutions; she was speaking to those who actually withheld their tithe. This statemement was written in 1890, prior to the establishment of self-supporting ministries within the Seventh-day Adventist Church, and therefore cannot be seen in the same light as later times, when there was the option of tithing to self-supporting ministries. We would point out that self-supporting ministries are just as God-ordained as are denominational ministries, and that Sister White, to show her strong support, became a member of the Board of Directors of Madison College to emphasize God's support for this form of work.

Argument Three. In 1 Corinthians 9, Paul clarifies that all who minister of holy things should live of the gospel (1 Corinthians 9:13-14); yet he made it clear that he did not accept tithes and offerings from the Corinthians.

But I have used none of these things: neither have I written these things, that it should be so done unto me (1 Corinthians 9:15).

Response. It is evident that in 1 Corinthians 9, Paul is talking about tithe to support the ministry, for to the Hebrews he wrote,

> And verily they that are of the sons of Levi, who receive the office of the priesthood, have a commandment to take tithes of the people according to the law, that is, of their brethren, though they come out of the loins of Abraham (Hebrews 7:5).

It is certain that it is those who preach the gospel who should live of the gospel. Many denominational ministers today are no longer preaching the gospel. Surely they are the ones who do not have the right to accept the tithes of God's people. However, those who are in lay ministries, who are preaching the gospel, have every right to such support. However, the issue here is not rights, but prudence. Those who look closely at 1 Corinthians 9:15 must take into account that Paul indeed, while in Corinth, was supported by the believers, and not only in Corinth, but also in other places. It would seem that the brethren in Philippi were the faithful supporters of Paul's ministry.

> Notwithstanding ye have well done, that ye did communicate with my affliction. Now ye Philippians know also, that in the beginning of the gospel, when I departed from Macedonia, no church communicated with me as concerning giving and receiving, but ye only. For even in Thessalonica ye sent once and again unto my necessity (Philippians 4:14-16).

That the Philippians continued to support Paul while he ministered in Corinth is clear.

> I robbed other churches, taking wages of them, to do you service. And when I was present with you, and wanted, I was chargeable to no man: for that which was lacking to me the brethren which came from Macedonia supplied: and in all things I have kept myself from being burdensome unto you, and so will I keep myself (2 Corinthians 11:8-9).

It would seem that there were some special problems in Corinth that led Paul to depend upon the generous, gracious, free and loving gifts of the Philippians rather than to accept anything from the Corinthians. This in no wise is an indication that the faithful ministers, be they denominational or self-supporting, should not be supported by the tithe.

While it might be wholly appropriate for faithful self-supporting ministers to accept tithe, it may be that because of the controversy that it has created, it is not wise to do so.

Now let us look at the opposite perspective, the understanding that tithes and offerings can appropriately be sent to sanctified self-supporting ministries.

Argument One. Sister White and others aided self-supporting ministries, even with tithe.

> I commend those sisters who have placed their tithe where it is most needed to help to do a work that is being left undone. If this matter is given publicity, it will create knowledge which would better be left as it is. I do not care to give publicity to this work which the Lord has appointed me to do, and others to do (Letter to Elder Watson, President of the Colorado Conference, January 22, 1905; also *Manuscript Releases*, volume 2, p.100).

Response. There is no evidence that this was to pay self-supporting workers; it was to support poorly-paid denominational workers.

Argument Two. Sister White actually urged that self-supporting workers should be paid from the tithe.

> There are minister's wives, Sisters Starr, Haskell, Wilson and Robinson, who have been devoted, earnest, whole-souled workers, giving Bible readings and praying with families, helping along by personal efforts just as successfully as their husbands. These women give their whole time, and are told that they receive nothing for their labors because their husbands receive their wages. I tell them to go forward and all such decisions shall be reversed. The Word says, "The laborer is worthy of his hire." When any such decision as this is made, I will in the name of the Lord, protest. I will feel it in my duty to create a fund from my tithe money, to pay these women who are accomplishing just as essential work as the ministers are doing; and this tithe I will reserve for work in the same line as that of the ministers, hunting for souls, fishing for souls (*Spalding and Magan Collection*, p. 117).

Response. These women were not ordinary self-supporting workers. They were actually the wives of ministers, and this should be taken into consideration.

Argument Three. The Bible and the Spirit of Prophecy designate the tithe for a special purpose, not a special group.

> I have had special instruction from the Lord that the tithe is for a special purpose, consecrated to God to sustain those who minister in the sacred work, as the Lord's chosen to do His work not only in sermonizing, but in ministering. They should understand all that this comprehends (*Manuscript Release*, volume 1, p. 187).

Response. This only applies to ordained, credentialed ministers. It does not refer to the lay ministry.

Argument Four. The Bible endorses paying self-supporting workers with tithe.

> Let the elders that rule well be counted worthy of double honor, especially those who labor in the Word and doctrine, for the Scripture saith, Thou shalt not muzzle the ox that treadeth out the corn. And, The laborer is worthy of his reward (I Timothy 5:17–18).

Response. While it might be appropriate in some cases to financially support elders, this does not say that such support should come from the tithe.

Argument Five. Sister White strongly urged Brethren Sutherland and Magan to solicit means for their self-supporting work.

> It is the privilege of these brethren to receive gifts from any of our people whom the Lord impresses to help (*Spalding and Magan Collection*, p. 422).

Response. It may be appropriate for self-supporting workers to receive offerings and donations, but they should not accept tithe.

Argument Six. The Bible calls withholding of tithes or offerings robbery to God; therefore, it is inconsistent to say that it would be wrong to apply tithe to worthy self-supporting workers, while it would be appropriate to apply offering.

> Will a man rob God? Yet ye have robbed me. But ye say, Wherein have we robbed thee? In tithes and offerings (Malachi 3:8).

Response. Malachi 3:10 only talks about the tithe being brought into the storehouse. Offerings are not included.

It would be possible for the authors to discuss the issue further, but this has given a sample of the various arguments and common responses.

We believe that the issue of the stewardship of an individual is a sacred trust. In the Day of Judgment, every human being will have to face the record of whether he has returned faithful tithes and offerings, and to where he has returned them. We believe the counsel of the Lord not to agitate this issue is wise. Men and women who are dedicated Seventh-day Adventists and who sincerely want to follow the Word of God have come to different conclusions. It may be that in the providence of God, as Sister White says, there have been some who have been called to do a different work with their tithe than others, so the Lord has convicted some in one way, and some in another. One thing is absolutely certain, that God has ordained both self-supporting and denominational ministry, and both are to play a mighty role in the finishing of the work of God on earth. Furthermore, it is important to recognize that only faithful ministers, from both self-supporting and denominational areas, will fulfill the gospel commission. God is looking for fidelity on the part of both. It is His will that faithful self-supporting workers unite with faithful denominational workers.

We believe the divisions that are being caused by the agitation of the tithe issue are not appropriate for God's end-time church, and the time has come to divide the church no more on this issue. Let all self-supporting and denominational ministries unite to encourage our people to return a faithful tithe and sacrificial offering unto the Lord. Thus His work can go forward and be completed, so that this world of sin and suffering can become part of the never-to-be-repeated history of the universe.

20

Suggestions for Laity Seeking to Fulfill
Their God-Given Responsibilities
in this Crisis Hour

As we have traveled around the world, we have discovered faithful laity wholly unprepared for the responsibilities and challenges of a period in history where church leadership has wittingly or unwittingly led the church into hierarchal organization. Most church members feel that they are impotent to do anything. Colin has noticed that frequently lay people believe that their pastors have the right to veto and to dominate the activities of the church. Thus, we are concluding this book with some helpful hints for laity, which also would be of great help to every minister seeking to play the role that God has called him to play in the last days of this world's history.

A. GENERAL COUNSEL

1. *Personal life:* With daily surrender of the will to Christ through prayer, Bible study and regular witnessing, seek to live an exemplary Christian life. Such a life will give you credibility as you seek to follow God's plan in your relationship to your fellow church members, pastor and conference leadership. Above all, true Christian authenticity is developed as the result of a consistent daily walk in the power and love of Christ.

2. *Remaining loyal to the pillars of the Adventist faith:* Avoid all speculative theology and prophetic interpretations, by which you quickly lose credibility in other matters of church life. Be slow, very slow, to embrace new and fascinating theories of men. Stay loyal to the foundations that have made Seventh-day Adventism what it is.

3. *Non-moral issues:* Choose carefully the issues that you stand for. Many areas of church life are not directly moral or spiritual issues, and though each member has the right and responsibility to express his opinions and his reasons for those

opinions, whether it be in board meetings or committee meetings, nevertheless, do not make them of such a consequence that they lead to a division amongst God's people.

4. *Matters of eternal consequence:* Never remain neutral on an issue that has eternal consequences. Neutrality in a time of spiritual crisis is the worst form of disloyalty to God. On the other hand, we must be sure that we present the issue in the most winning but direct way, that all might understand.

5. *Negligence of duty:* Remember that you will stand in judgment for any neglect of duty. Make your witness central to your whole life as a responsible and faithful member of the church.

6. *Following men:* Do not allow yourself to follow any human being, even if he seems to be right most of the time. Carefully check even the most respected man's judgments and opinions. Many who have been drawn into following even faithful men have been lost by continuing to follow when those individuals have moved away from truth and righteousness.

7. *The errors of others:* Do not assume someone is deliberately falling into doctrinal errors; they may be ignorant of the truth. Gently seek to help them understand the truth. Personal attacks will not help, nor will talking about these errors with other members of the church. Only after you have carefully and lovingly sought to explain the error to the person, and the person has not responded, should you speak of the error to others.

8. *Financial support:* Be a sacrificial financial supporter of every worthy cause that will forward the gospel in your church. Refuse to support any project, financially or otherwise, that you know is contrary to the purposes of God.

9. *Removal from office:* Do not express hurt or ill feelings if you are not chosen to continue in a particular office. That applies even if you know it is your stand for truth and righteousness that has led to the decision made.

10. *Resigning from church office:* Many laity who are under pressure because of their stand for truth have resigned from their church office. That is a serious mistake. God may want you there for such a time as this. Do not consider the pressure upon you; rather, look to Christ, Who is able to sustain you, and ask Him to keep you in that office or some other office as long as you can be

a blessing to the church and its membership. It is God's decision, not yours, whether you continue in office. Remember, all things work together for good to them that love the Lord.

11. *Rendering reproof:* Love will not allow someone to continue in error without rendering entreaties and reproofs. Make sure you have prayed earnestly for love for the one in error before taking on such a heavy responsibility, yet never neglect that responsibility.

12. *Another member in error:* Speak directly to the one in error. Do not make a scandal of the situation by talking about it with other church members.

13. *Error or sin within the church:* Protest, kindly but firmly.

B. COUNSEL IN RELATION TO LOCAL CHURCH AFFAIRS

1. *Church nominating committee:* The importance of the church nominating committee is such that it is essential that only men and women of the highest spiritual maturity, men and women who are truly committed to God's Word and His truth, be chosen to be on it. These committee members choose the officers of the church, and that is critical to the spiritual growth and development of the church. Nominate and vote for only such members.

2. *Remove senior roles:* Do not participate in the modern practice of selecting senior elders, senior deacons, senior deaconesses; such sets one apart from the others, and leads away from the counsel of Jesus, "All ye are brethren." Allow the elders, deacons and deaconesses to meet together informally and take turns in leadership roles in their respective responsibilities.

3. *Chairmanship of board and business meetings:* Have the elders share the chairmanship of the church board meetings and business meetings, allowing different perspectives to be presented, and leadership of such a nature that no one is in a position to exercise a kingly role.

4. *Domination of church decisions:* Let no man or woman be allowed the right to dominate the decisions of the church. Do not even allow a small group of men or women that right. It is not uncommon to have in a church a small power group that somehow, perhaps because of the acquiescence or weakness of most of

the members, are able to channel the direction of the church any way they deem appropriate. Those who allow such to happen are abdicating a God-given responsibility.

5. *Responsibilities of elders:* Remember that the New Testament order calls for the elders to be the spiritual leaders of the local church congregation. They are responsible for the spiritual growth of the church, and the nurturing of new members. They are to care for those who are backsliding and weakening spiritually.

6. *The roles of deacons and deaconesses:* Here again, reestablish the God-given roles of the deacons and the deaconesses. They are responsible to care for the needy in the congregation, to offer counsel in family issues, to visit the sick, the infirm, and the shut-ins, and offer to them the spiritual blessings that they need.

7. *Inservice training of members:* Church leaders, especially elders, are responsible for having an ongoing inservice training program to encourage witnessing and outreach in the church. This is especially important for the children and youth of the church, but it is also important for new members and even older members who are unaccustomed to witnessing about their faith.

8. *Have an active prayer and testimony meeting each week:* Let the prayer and testimony meeting have such a power that church members are attracted to it. Let the great truths of the Adventist faith be retold and repeated, and let the church members have the privilege of sharing witnessing experiences at each midweek prayer meeting.

9. *Church Manual:* Do not use the Church Manual in dealing with church matters. Make sure that the Bible and the Spirit of Prophecy alone are the basis of the decision-making in the church.

10. *Disfellowshiping:* Recognizing that those who continue in deliberate sin or doctrinal apostasy bring great impotency to the church, the church board members, especially the elders, have a responsibility to deal with these issues. These issues must be dealt with in love and concern, entreating the ones who have fallen, recognizing that we ourselves could fall. Nevertheless, should there be a clear failure to respond to the entreaties, it is essential that the hand of fellowship be withdrawn from such a person. How-

ever, consider that there are only two valid reasons for disfellow-shipping a member—doctrinal apostasy and continuance in open sin.

11. *Accepting members into the church:* Do not accept a new member or a transfer member into the church without a full investigation of his or her commitment to the truth of the three angels and to a life of righteous living. It should be the practice of every church, and the expectation of anyone seeking membership in the church, that such a one will have the opportunity to affirm or reaffirm his or her faith in the great Advent message before being brought into church fellowship.

12. *Church board:* It may be wise for small churches not to choose a church board, but to allow the church business meetings to act in all matters pertaining to church decision-making.

13. *Require regular quarterly church business meetings:* Many churches today rarely have business meetings, partly due to the fact that few attend. However, the work of the local church, its outreach and its thrust into the community, should be carefully and prayerfully studied by its members on a regular basis. Therefore, these regularly-called business meetings should become an important part of church life.

14. *Attend all business meetings:* Sometimes laity have complained that they have no influence anymore because they are no longer part of the church board. Indeed, even more important than the church board, which acts between business meetings on behalf of the church, is the church business meeting, which supersedes the power of the church board. It is important to redress anything that may have been voted by the church board at a church business meeting. All faithful members should regularly attend such business meetings, and should actively participate in them. It is essential that you plan to stay right through a church board or business meeting, no matter how long it is, for important items, which could have crucial consequences in the church, are often raised toward the end of meetings.

15. *Responsibility at business meetings:* Make it a plan to place before the business meeting those issues that will uphold truth and righteousness and forward the missionary outreach and witness of the church. If the matter is one of great consequence, make sure you have enough copies of your recommendation or

amendment that you can pass them out to all members. Also, be sure that you take the time to carefully articulate the issues that are at stake. Always, of course, present your motion in Christian courtesy.

16. *Motion-making:* On any important issue, never begin your address with "I think," but rather with "I move." Seek to put a motion on the table to address the issue. When seconded, ask to speak to the motion. If a motion is already on the floor, articulate the reasons for your support or non-support of the motion.

17. *Board of elders:* Even in large churches, a board of elders should *not* function in a local church, for this allows decision-making to be in the hands of a few people. Do not allow decisions rightly reserved for the board meeting to be handled by a board of elders.

18. *Conference offering list:* Support heartily all worthwhile offerings and projects presented by the conference. Should there be one that cannot rightly be supported, the church board has a responsibility to choose another project for the offering.

19. *Preaching plan:* The weekly preaching plan should not be in the hands of one man, even if he is the pastor. It should be in the hands of the church board, which should not only choose the speakers for each week, but also be responsible for making sure that every year the great pillars of our faith are covered thoroughly.

20. *Church ownership:* Do everything possible to get the ownership of the church back into the hands of the local congregation. This is essential in this day of financial uncertainty and great apostasy.

C. COUNSEL REGARDING RELATIONSHIPS WITH CHURCH PASTORS

1. *Pastor support:* Wherever you possibly can, support your pastor. He has a lonely road. Do everything you can to uphold him.

2. *Pray for your pastor:* Prayer is often far more powerful than criticism. That does not mean that you overlook the errors of your pastor, but pray earnestly that God will guide and sustain him.

3. *Pastor in error:* Work kindly but firmly with a pastor in error. Seek to help him see where his presentations are not consistent with the Bible and the Spirit of Prophecy, but do not allow the first thread of aberration from truth to pass unaddressed. Constantly encourage and uphold a pastor who is faithful to truth and righteousness; there will probably be others attacking him.

4. *Pastoral duties:* Screen your pastor from all significant church duties which should be carried out by the elders, deacons, deaconesses, et cetera, allowing the pastor to engage primarily in evangelistic and soul-winning endeavors.

5. *Fully support crusades and seminars:* It is discouraging to a pastor when his members do not support his evangelistic outreach. Be faithful in supporting such endeavors, and you yourself will be blessed as the great truths of the gospel are brought back to your attention. If you have children, it will be a great opportunity for spiritual education for them. Make sure that at least one long crusade or seminar, covering several months, is held each year.

6. *Divine service:* Expect your minister not to simply preach *pleasant* truth, but *present* truth. That should be non-negotiable.

7. *When error continues to be preached:* The board has a responsibility to shield the flock from the presentation of error. The elders should dialogue with the pastor, making it clear that their church is looking for present truth, and that alone is acceptable to be preached in the pulpit. This means that the board will not allow generalized sermons to dominate the spiritual food presented in the pulpit, even if they do not contain error.

8. *Board meeting:* Under no circumstances should the pastor veto the decision of a board or business meeting. Indeed, it would be well for the pastor not to spend his valuable time in attendance at such meetings unless it be by special request. His role in the preparation of new members is far more important.

9. *Nominating committee:* Under no circumstances should the pastor sit even as an advisor on the nominating committee. His presence is likely to dominate or overly influence nominating committee decisions. Never allow a pastor or church board to intervene between the nominating committee's report and its presentation to the church as a whole.

10. *Lab 1, Lab 2 and NLP:* It is important to determine whether your pastor has been involved in Lab 1, Lab 2 and NLP. If he has, you need to dialogue with him personally, helping him to see the danger of using the techniques that he has learned.

11. *Pastors who refuse to preach truth:* If, after every effort has been made to encourage your pastor to preach that which is meat in due season for the congregation, he still refuses, it is the responsibility of the lay leadership and the church as a whole to ask him not to preach any more in the church. As far as possible, this should be done in consultation with conference leadership, but the elders of the church and other leaders have a responsibility before God not to allow error to continue to be presented to the flock, irrespective of the conference's response.

D. COUNSEL IN RELATIONSHIP TO THE CONFERENCE AND CONFERENCE LEADERSHIP

1. *Support the conference:* Do all you can to support your conference activities wherever it is conscientiously possible.

2. *Conference constituency meetings:* Take conference constituency meetings very seriously. Choose prayerfully as representatives only laity who are totally committed to God, and who are consecrated men and women with deep perception, of and alertness to the issues of today.

3. *Delegates to conference sessions:* Prepare in advance important motions or suggested amendments, and make sure you have these printed out in sufficient quantity for all the delegates.

4. *Choice of conference officers and committees:* Make the choice of conference officers and committees very prayerfully, for the men and women who are chosen for various roles must be men and women of God, who love the truth. Be earnest in seeking the best leadership possible.

5. *Presenting a motion or a proposed amendment:* Do not allow any chairman to refuse you the right to speak to a motion or a prepared amendment. This is your God-given responsibility.

6. *Delegates at conference sessions:* If you have been chosen to be a delegate at a conference session, plan to stay right through until the end of the session. You have a responsibility to your church and to God to be there for every section of the meeting.

7. *General Conference recommendations:* Remember that the General Conference recommendations do not have to be adopted. Consider them carefully. You may decide to wholeheartedly support, to seek an amendment, or to vote against that recommendation.

8. *Undue conference pressure:* Do not ever yield to intimidation or threatening, even if it comes from the conference. Always do what you know is right, not just what is convenient.

9. *Meetings with church members at the request of conference leaders:* In any such formal meetings it is altogether appropriate to choose one of the lay leaders of the church to chair the meeting. A member of the conference is there to serve the needs of the church, not the church to serve the needs of the conference.

10. *Choosing a new pastor:* Ask that the conference give the members of your church the opportunity to make major input into the choice of any minister who will pastor your church. Explain the exact expectations that you have for such a pastor, especially in respect to his loyalty to God's truth. It is wise to carefully interview the pastor *before* he is appointed, making clear the church's expectations of him.

11. *Commending conference:* Be quick by voice and pen to commend conference leadership or committees when they make decisions which meet the approval of God's Word. It is important not only to contact leaders when we disapprove of what has taken place, but also when we approve of their actions. Above all, let everything be done in true Christian love and courtesy, so that the reforms that you are seeking to achieve and the hastening of the coming of the Lord might not be inhibited by a wrong approach.

Appendix A

A Declaration of the Fundamental Principles Taught and Practiced by the Seventh-day Adventists (1872)

<u>FUNDAMENTAL PRINCIPLES</u>

In presenting to the public this synopsis of our faith, we wish to have it distinctly understood that we have no articles of faith, creed, or discipline, aside from the Bible. We do not put forth this as having any authority with our people, nor is it designed to secure uniformity among them, as a system of faith, but is a brief statement of what is, and has been, with great unanimity, held by them.

We often find it necessary to meet inquiries on this subject, and sometimes to correct false statements circulated against us, and to remove erroneous impressions which have obtained with those who have not had an opportunity to become acquainted with our faith and practice. Our only object is to meet this necessity.

As Seventh-day Adventists, we desire simply that our position shall be understood; and we are more solicitous for this because there are many who call themselves Adventists who hold views with which we can have no sympathy, some of which, we think, are subversive of the plainest and most important principles set forth in the word of God.

As compared with other Adventists, Seventh-day Adventists differ from one class in believing in the unconscious state of the dead, and the final destruction of the unrepentant wicked; from another in believing in the perpetuity of the law of God as summarily contained in the ten commandments, in the operation of the Holy Spirit in the church, and in setting no times for the advent to occur; from all in the observance of the seventh day of the week as the Sabbath of the Lord, and in many applications of the prophetic scriptures.

With these remarks, we ask the attention of the reader to the following propositions which aim to be a concise statement of the more prominent features of our faith.

DECLARATION OF PRINCIPLES

1. That there is one God, a personal, spiritual being, the creator of all things, omnipotent, and eternal, infinite in wisdom, holiness, justice, goodness, truth, and mercy; unchangeable, and everywhere present by His representative, the Holy Spirit. Ps. 139:7

2. That there is one Lord Jesus Christ, the Son of the Eternal Father, the one by whom God created all things, and by whom they do consist; that He took on Him the nature of the seed of Abraham for the redemption of our fallen race; that He dwelt among men, full of grace and truth, lived our example, died our sacrifice, and was raised for our justification.

He ascended on high to be our only mediator in the sanctuary in Heaven, where, with His own blood, He makes atonement for our sins; which atonement so far from being made on the cross, which was by the offering of the sacrifice, is the very last portion of His work as priest according to the example of the Levitical priesthood, which foreshadowed and prefigured the ministry of our Lord in Heaven. See Lev. 16; Heb. 8:4,5; 9:6,7; etc.

3. That the Holy Scriptures, of the Old and New Testaments, were given by inspiration of God, contain a full revelation of His will to man, and are the only infallible rule of faith and practice.

4. That Baptism is an ordinance of the Christian church, to follow faith and repentance, an ordinance by which we commemorate the resurrection of Christ, as by this act we show our faith in his burial and resurrection, and through that, of the resurrection of all the saints at the last day; and that no other mode fitly represents these facts than that which the Scriptures prescribe, namely, immersion. Rom. 6:3–6; Col. 2:12.

5. That the new birth comprises the entire change necessary to fit us for the kingdom of God, and consists of two parts: first, a moral change wrought by conversion and a Christian life; second, a physical change at the second coming of Christ, whereby, if dead, we are raised incorruptible, and if living, are changed to immortality in a moment, in the twinkling of an eye. John 3:3,5; Luke 20:36.

6.We believe that prophecy is a part of God's revelation to man; that it is included in that scripture which is profitable for instruction, 2 Tim. 3:16; that it is designed for us and our children, Deut. 29:29; that so far from being enshrouded in impenetrable mystery, it is that which especially constitutes the word of God a lamp to our feet and a light to our path, Ps. 119:105; 2 Pet. 2:19; that a blessing is pronounced upon those who study it, Rev. 1:1–3; and that, consequently, it is to be understood by the people of God sufficiently to show them their position in the world's history, and the special duties required at their hands.

7. That the world's history from specified dates in the past, the rise and fall of empires, and chronological succession of events down to the setting up of God's everlasting kingdom, are outlined in numerous great chains of prophecy; and that these prophecies are now all fulfilled except the closing scenes.

8. That the doctrine of the world's conversion and temporal millennium is a fable of these last days, calculated to lull men into a state of carnal security, and cause them to be overtaken by the great day of the Lord as by a thief in the night; that the second coming of Christ is to precede, not follow, the millennium; for until the Lord appears the papal power, with all its abominations, is to continue, the wheat and tares grow together, and evil men and seducers wax worse and worse, as the word of God declares.

9. The mistake of Adventists in 1844 pertained to the nature of the event then to transpire, not to the time; that no prophetic period is given to reach to the second advent, but that the longest one, the two thousand and three hundred days of Dan. 8:14, terminated in that year, and brought us to an event called the cleansing of the sanctuary.

10. That the sanctuary of the new covenant is the tabernacle of God in Heaven, of which Paul speaks in Hebrews 8, and onward, of which our Lord, as great High Priest, is minister; that this sanctuary is the antitype of the Mosaic tabernacle, and that the priestly work of our Lord, connected therewith, is the antitype of the work of the Jewish priests of the former dispensation. Heb. 8:1–5; etc.

That this is the sanctuary to be cleansed at the end of the 2300 days, what is termed its cleansing being in this case, as in the type, simply the entrance of the high priest into the most holy place, to finish the round of service connected therewith, by blotting out and removing from the sanctuary the sins which had been transferred to it by means of the ministration of the first apartment, Heb. 9:22,23; and that this work, in the antitype, commencing in 1844, occupies a brief but indefinite space, at the conclusion of which the work of mercy for the world is finished.

11. That God's moral requirements are the same upon all men in all dispensations; that these are summarily contained in the commandments spoken by Jehovah from Sinai, engraved on the tables of stone, and deposited in the ark, which was in consequence called the "ark of the covenant," or testament. Num. 10:33; Heb. 9:4; etc; that this law is immutable and perpetual, being a transcript of the tables deposited in the ark in the true sanctuary on high, which is also, for the same reason, called the ark of God's testament; for under the sounding of the seventh trumpet we are told that "the temple of God was opened in Heaven, and there was seen in His temple the ark of His testament." Rev.11:19.

12. That the fourth commandment of this law requires that we devote the seventh day of each week, commonly called Saturday, to abstinence from our own labor, and to the performance of sacred and religious duties; that this is the only weekly Sabbath known to the Bible, being the day that was set apart before paradise was lost, Gen. 2:2,3; and which will be observed in paradise restored, Isa. 66:22, 23;

That the facts upon which the Sabbath institution is based confine it to the seventh day, as they are not true of any other day; and that the terms, Jewish Sabbath and Christian Sabbath as applied to the weekly rest-day, are names of human invention, unscriptural in fact, and false in meaning.

13. That as the man of sin, the Papacy, has thought to change times and laws (the laws of God), Dan 7:25, and has misled almost all Christendom in regard to the fourth commandment; we find a prophecy of a reform in this respect to be wrought among believers just before the coming of Christ. Isa. 56:1,2; 1 Pet. 1:5; Rev. 14:12; etc.

14. That as the natural or carnal heart is at enmity with God and His law, this enmity can be subdued only by a radical transformation of the affections, the exchange of unholy for holy principles; that this transformation follows repentance and faith, is the special work of the Holy Spirit, and constitutes regeneration or conversion.

15. That as all have violated the law of God, and cannot of themselves render obedience to His just requirements, we are dependent on Christ, first, for justification from our past offenses, and secondly, for grace whereby to render acceptable obedience to His holy law in time to come.

16. That the Spirit of God was promised to manifest itself in the church through certain gifts, enumerated especially in 2 Cor. 12 and Eph. 4; that these gifts are not designed to supersede, or take the place of the Bible, which is sufficient to make us wise unto salvation, any more than the Bible can take the place of the Holy Spirit.

That in specifying the various channels of its operation, that Spirit has simply made provision for its own existence and presence with the people of God to the end of time, to lead to an understanding of the word which it had inspired, to convince of sin, and work a transformation in the heart and life; and that those who deny to the Spirit its place and operation, do plainly deny that part of the Bible which assigns to it this work and position.

17. That God, in accordance with His uniform dealing with the race, sends forth a proclamation of the approach of the second advent of Christ; that this work is symbolized by the three mes-

sages of Rev. 14, the last one bringing to view the work of reform on the law of God, that His people may acquire a complete readiness for that event.

18. That the time of the cleansing of the sanctuary (see proposition 10), synchronizing with the time of the proclamation of the third message, is a time of the investigative judgement, first with reference to the dead, and at the close of probation with reference to the living; to determine who of the myriads now sleeping in the dust of the earth are worthy of a part in the first resurrection, and who of its living multitudes are worthy of translation—points which must be determined before the Lord appears.

19. That the grave, whither we all tend, expressed by the Hebrew sheol, and the Greek hades, is a place of darkness in which there is no work, device, wisdom, or knowledge. Eccl. 9:10.

20. That the state to which we are reduced by death is one of silence, inactivity, and entire unconsciousness. Ps. 146:4; Eccl. 9:5,6; Dan. 12:2; etc.

21. That out of this prison house of the grave of mankind are to be brought by a bodily resurrection; the righteous having part in the first resurrection, which takes place at the second advent of Christ, the wicked in the second resurrection, which takes place a thousand years thereafter. Rev. 20:4–6.

22. That at the last trump, the living righteous are to be changed in a moment, in the twinkling of an eye, and with the resurrected righteous are to be caught up to meet the Lord in the air, so forever to be with God.

23. That these immortalized ones are then taken to Heaven, to the New Jerusalem, the Father's house in which there are many mansions, John 14:1–3; where they reign with Christ a thousand years, judging the world and fallen angels, that is, apportioning the punishment to be executed upon them at the close of the one thousand years; Rev. 20:4; 1 Cor. 6:2,3.

That during this time the earth lies in a desolate and chaotic condition, Jer. 4:20–27; described, as in the beginning by the Greek term *abussos*, bottomless pit (Septuagint of Genesis 1:2); and that here Satan is confined during the thousand years, Rev.20:1,2; here finally destroyed, Rev. 20:10; Mal. 4:1; the theater of the ruin he has wrought in the universe, being appropriately made for a time his gloomy prison house, and then the place of his final execution.

24. That at the end of the thousand years, the Lord descends with his people and the new Jerusalem, Rev. 21:2; the wicked dead are raised and come up upon the surface of the yet unrenewed earth, and gather about the city, the camp of the saints, Rev. 20:9; and fire comes down from God out of heaven and devours them. They are then consumed root and branch, Mal. 4:1; becoming as though they had not been. Obad. 15,16.

In this everlasting destruction from the presence of the Lord, 2 Thess. 1:9; the wicked meet the everlasting punishment threatened against them, Matt. 25:46. This is the perdition of un-godly men, the fire which consumes them being the fire for which "the heavens and the earth which are now," are kept in store, which shall melt even the elements with its intensity, and purge the earth from the deepest stains of the curse of sin. 2 Pet. 3:7–12.

25. That a new heavens and earth shall spring by the power of God from the ashes of the old, to be, with the New Jerusalem for its metropolis and capital, the eternal inheritance of the saints, the place where the righteous shall evermore dwell. 2 Pet. 3:13; Ps. 37:11,29; Mat. 5:5.

Appendix B

Fundamental Beliefs of Seventh-day Adventists Church Manual (1932)

Seventh-day Adventists hold certain fundamental beliefs, the principal features of which, together with a portion of the Scriptural references upon which they are based, may be summarized as follows:

1. That the Holy Scriptures of the Old and New Testaments were given by inspiration of God, contain an all-sufficient revelation of His will to men, and are the only unerring rule of faith and practice. 2 Tim. 3:15–17.

2. That the Godhead, or Trinity, consists of the Eternal Father, a personal, spiritual Being, omnipotent, omnipresent, omniscient, infinite in wisdom and love; the Lord Jesus Christ, the Son of the Eternal Father, through whom all things were created and through whom the salvation of the redeemed hosts will be accomplished; the Holy Spirit, the third person of the Godhead, the great regenerating power in the work of redemption. Matt. 28:19.

3. That Jesus Christ is very God, being of the same nature and essence as the Eternal Father. While retaining His divine nature, He took upon Himself the nature of the human family, lived on the earth as a man, exemplified in His life as our example the principles of righteousness, attested His relationship to God by many mighty miracles, died for our sins on the cross, was raised from the dead, and ascended to the Father, where He ever lives to make intercession for us. John 1:1, 14; Heb. 2:9–18; 8:1,2; 4:14–16; 7:25.

4. That every person in order to obtain salvation must experience the new birth; that this comprises an entire transformation of life and character by the re-creative power of God through faith in the Lord Jesus Christ. John 3:16; Matt. 18:3; Acts 2:37–39.

5. That baptism is an ordinance of the Christian church, and should follow repentance and forgiveness of sins. By its observance faith is shown in the death, burial, and resurrection of Christ. That the proper form of baptism is by immersion. Rom. 6:1-6; Acts 16:30-33.

6. That the will of God as it relates to moral conduct is comprehended in His law of ten commandments; that these are great moral, unchangeable precepts, binding upon all men in every age. Ex. 20:1-17.

7. That the fourth commandment of this unchangeable law requires the observance of the seventh-day Sabbath. This holy institution is at the same time a memorial of creation and a sign of sanctification, a sign of the believer's rest from his own works of sin, and his entrance into the rest of soul which Jesus promises to those who come to Him. Gen. 2:1-3; Ex. 20:8-11; 31:12-17; Heb. 4:1-10.

8. That the law of ten commandments points out sin, the penalty of which is death. The law cannot save the transgressor from his sin, nor impart power to keep him from sinning. In infinite love and mercy, God provides a way whereby this may be done. He furnishes a substitute, even Christ the righteous one, to die in man's stead, making "Him to be sin for us, who knew no sin; that we might be made the righteousness of God in Him." 2 Cor. 5:21. That one is justified, not by obedience to the law, but by the grace that is in Christ Jesus. By accepting Christ, man is reconciled to God, justified by His blood for the sins of the past, and saved from the power of sin by His indwelling life. Thus the gospel becomes "the power of God unto salvation to every one that believeth." This experience is wrought by the divine agency of the Holy Spirit, who convinces of sin and leads to the Sin Bearer, inducting the believer into the new-covenant relationship, where the law of God is written on his heart, and through the enabling power of the indwelling Christ, his life is brought into conformity to the divine precepts. The honor and merit of this wonderful transformation being wholly to Christ. 1 John 3:4; Rom. 7:7; 3:20; Eph. 2:8-10; 1 John 2:1,2; Rom. 5:8-10; Gal. 2:20; Eph. 3:17; Heb. 8:8-12.

9. That God only hath immortality. Mortal man possesses a nature inherently sinful and dying. Immortality and eternal life come only through the gospel, and are bestowed as the free gift of God at the second advent of Jesus Christ our Lord. 1 Tim. 6:15,16; 1 Cor. 15:51–55.

10. That the condition of man in death is one of unconsciousness. That all men, good and evil alike, remain in the grave from death to the resurrection. Eccl. 9:5,6; Ps. 146:3,4; John 5:28,29.

11. That there shall be a resurrection both of the just and of the unjust. The resurrection of the just will take place at the second coming of Christ; the resurrection of the unjust will take place a thousand years later, at the close of the millennium. John 5:28,29; 1 Thess. 4:13–18; Rev. 20:5–10.

12. That the finally impenitent, including Satan, the author of sin, will, by the fires of the last day, be reduced to a state of nonexistence, becoming as though they had not been, thus purging the universe of God of sin and sinners. Rom. 6:23; Mal. 4:1–3; Rev. 20:9,10; Obadiah 16.

13. That no prophetic period is given in the Bible to reach to the second advent, but that the longest one, the 2300 days of Daniel 8:14, terminated in 1844, and brought us to an event called the cleansing of the sanctuary.

14. That the true sanctuary, of which the tabernacle on earth was a type, is the temple of God in heaven, of which Paul speaks in Hebrews 8 and onward, and of which the Lord Jesus, as our great High Priest, is minister; and that the priestly work of our Lord is the antitype of the work of the Jewish priests of the former dispensation; that this heavenly sanctuary is the one to be cleansed at the end of the 2300 days of Daniel 8:14; its cleansing being, as in the type, a work of judgment, beginning with the entrance of Christ as the High Prist upon the judgment phase of His ministry in the heavenly sanctuary, foreshadowed in the earthly service of cleansing the sanctuary on the day of atonement. This work of judgment in the heavenly sanctuary began in 1844. Its completion will close human probation.

15. That God, in the time of the judgment and in accordance with His uniform dealing with the human family in warning them of coming events vitally affecting their destiny (Amos 3:6,7), sends forth a proclamation of the approach of the second advent of

Christ; that this work is symbolized by the three angels of Revelation 14; and that their threefold message brings to view a work of reform to prepare a people to meet Him at His coming.

16. That the time of the cleansing of the sanctuary, synchronizing with the period of the proclamation of the message of Revelation 14, is a time of investigative judgment, first with reference to the dead, and secondly, with reference to the living. This investigative judgment determines who of the myriads sleeping in the dust of the earth are worthy of a part in the first resurrection, and who of its living multitudes are worthy of translation. 1 Peter 4:17,18; Dan. 7:9,10; Rev. 14:6,7; Luke 20:35.

17. That the followers of Christ should be a godly people, not adopting the unholy maxims nor conforming to the unrighteous ways of the world, not loving its sinful pleasures nor countenancing its follies. That the believer should recognize his body as the temple of the Holy Spirit, and that therefore he should clothe that body in neat, modest, dignified apparel. Further, that in eating and drinking and in his entire course of conduct he should shape his life as becometh a follower of the meek and lowly Master. Thus the believer will be led to abstain from all intoxicating drinks, tobacco, and other narcotics, and to avoid every body- and soul-defiling habit and practice. 1 Cor. 3:16,17; 9:25; 10:31; 1 Tim. 2:9,10; 1 John 2:6.

18. That the divine principle of tithes and offerings for the support of the gospel is an acknowledgment of God's ownership in our lives, and that we are stewards who must render account to Him of all that He has committed to our possession. Lev. 27:30; Mal. 3:8–12; Matt. 23:23; 1 Cor. 9:9–14, 2 Cor. 9:6–15.

19. That God has placed in His church the gifts of the Holy Spirit, as enumerated in 1 Corinthians 12 and Ephesians 4. That these gifts operate in harmony with the divine principles of the Bible, and are given for the perfecting of the saints, the work of the ministry, the edifying of the body of Christ. Rev. 12:17; 19:10; 1 Cor. 1:5–7.

20. That the second coming of Christ is the great hope of the church, the grand climax of the gospel and plan of salvation. His coming will be literal, personal, and visible. Many important events will be associated with His return, such as the resurrection of the dead, the destruction of the wicked, the purification of the earth,

the reward of the righteous, the establishment of His everlasting kingdom. The almost complete fulfillment of various lines of prophecy, particularly those found in the books of Daniel and the Revelation, and existing conditions in the physical, social, industrial, political, and religious worlds, indicates that Christ's coming "is near, even at the doors." The exact time of the event has not been foretold. Believers are exhorted to be ready, for "in such an hour as ye think not, the Son of man" will be revealed. Luke 21:25,27; 17:26–30; John 14:1–3; Acts 1:9–11; Rev. 1:7; Heb. 9:28; James 5: 1–8; Joel 3:9–16; 2 Tim. 3:1–5; Dan. 7:27; Matt. 24:36,44.

21. That the millennial reign of Christ covers the period between the first and the second resurrection, during which time the saints of all ages will live with their blessed Redeemer in heaven. At the end of the millennium, the Holy City with all the saints will descend to the earth. The wicked, raised in the second resurrection, will go up on the breadth of the earth with Satan at their head to compass the camp of the saints, when fire will come down from God out of heaven and devour them. In the conflagration which destroys Satan and his host, the earth itself will be regenerated and cleansed from the effects of the curse. Thus the universe of God will be purified from the foul blot of sin. Revelation 20; Zech. 14:1–4; 2 Peter 3:7–10.

22. That God will make all things new. The earth, restored to its pristine beauty, will become forever the abode of the saints of the Lord. The promise to Abraham, that through Christ, the Lord will reign supreme, and every creature which is in heaven and on earth and under the earth, and such as are in the sea will ascribe blessing and honor and glory and power unto Him that sitteth upon the throne and unto the Lamb forever and ever. Gen. 13:14–17; Rom. 4:13; Heb. 11:8–16; Matt 5:5; Isaiah 35; Rev. 21:1–7; Dan 7:27; Rev. 5:13.—*Seventh-day Adventist Year Book, 1931.*

Appendix C
Outline of Examination for Baptism
1932 Church Manual

1. Do you believe in the existence of God as a personal being, who is our heavenly Father?

2. Do you believe in the Lord Jesus as the eternal Son of God, as the Saviour and Redeemer of mankind? Have you fully accepted Him as your personal Saviour, and the salvation He offers through grace?

3. Do you believe in the Holy Spirit and in His work in leading to repentance and obedience to all God's requirements?

4. Do you accept the Bible as the inspired word of God, and will you study faithfully its teachings and by the grace of God practice them in your life?

5. Do you believe in conversion as an experience spoken of by Christ as the new birth?

6. Have you confessed your sins to God, as far as they have been made known to you; and have you on your part, as far as in you lies, tried to make wrongs right with your fellow men?

7. Do you claim by faith in Christ that God for Christ's sake has forgiven your past sins, and that He is yours and you are His?

8. So far as you have studied and investigated the doctrines as taught by the Seventh-day Adventist denomination, do you believe in and accept them?

9. Do you believe in the second coming of Jesus, which is taught in the Scriptures as the blessed hope, and that this event is soon to take place, and that you should prepare for His coming by being purified from sin and evil?

10. Recognizing obedience as the fruit of faithful love, do you believe that all ten of the commandments as spoken by the Lord are still binding, and by God's grace will you keep those commandments, the fourth with the rest, observing as sacred the seventh-day Sabbath from sundown Friday to sundown Saturday?

11. Do you recognize the fact that God claims one-tenth of all our substance as His for the support of His work in advancing the gospel of Christ; and will you faithfully render to Him His own— the tithe and offerings in the support of the worldwide work of the church?

12. Do you believe that man by nature is mortal, and that immortality and eternal life come only through the gospel and are bestowed as the free gift of God through Christ at His second coming?

13. Do you believe that we are living in the time of the investigative judgment, which began in 1844, and that Christ, as our High Priest, is closing His ministry in the most holy apartment of the heavenly sanctuary in preparation for His coming?

14. Do you believe that the closing gospel message is now going to the world and will be finished in this generation; and will you use your means, as God impresses you, your time, and your talents, that others may be blessed with the light of truth that has brought blessing and light to you?*

15. Will you seek to build up the interests of the church by attendance at its meetings and ordinances, and by adding your influence to extend its work while the church, on their part, exercise their watchcare over you?

16. Do you understand the principles of Christian temperance as taught by Seventh-day Adventists, and will you carry out those principles in your life, abstaining from the use of intoxicating

---

* Those conducting Bible classes should make sure that thorough instruction is given, not only in the points mentioned above, but in every other doctrine and phase of present truth.

liquors, tobacco in all its forms, swine's flesh, and all other unclean foods and habit-forming drugs?*

17. In matters of dress will you follow the Bible rule of plainness
and simplicity, abstaining from the wearing of gold as ornaments
and costly array, observing the principles of modesty and Christian dignity?

18. Do you believe the Bible doctrine of "spiritual gifts" in the
church, and do you believe in the gift of the Spirit of prophecy
which has been manifested in the remnant church through the
ministry and writings of Mrs. E. G. White?

19. Do you believe in baptism by immersion, and is it your desire,
by going forward in this ordinance, to manifest your faith in the
saving grace of the Lord Jesus Christ?

20. Do you, by going forward in baptism, thus declare that from
henceforth you will have no part in such soul-destroying amusements as card playing, theater going, dancing, and all other enter-
tainments and amusements which tend to deaden and destroy the
spiritual life and perceptions?

21. Will you submit to the decisions of the body of the church in
matters of church discipline?

---

* In preparing candidates for baptism, instruction should be given as to the harmful effects of
such condiments as tea, coffee, and other harmful beverages.

Appendix D
1946 Baptismal Vows

1. Do you accept all the Bible as the inspired word of God, and do you take it as your only rule of faith? Is it your purpose to ever walk according to its teachings? 2 Tim. 3:16, 17; Acts 20:32

2. Have you received the Lord Jesus Christ as your personal Savior for salvation from sin, for a real change of heart, and will you permit Him by the Holy Spirit to live in you daily? John 1:12, 13; Gal 2:20

3. Have you repented of, and confessed, all known sin to God: and do you believe that He for Christ's sake has forgiven you: and as far as possible have you tried to make matters right with your fellow men? 1 John 1:9; Matt. 5:23-26; Eze. 33:15.

4. Is it your purpose, by the grace of God, to live a true Christian life, by surrendering all—soul, body, and spirit—to God, to do His will in all things, and to keep all the commandments of God? Rom. 12:1; Col. 3:17; Rev. 14:12

5. Will you seek to maintain a true spiritual experience by the daily study of God's Word, and prayer: and will you endeavor by your consistent life and personal effort to win souls to Christ?

6. Do you believe and accept the great truths of the Word of God concerning the personal, visible, literal, imminent return of Christ (Acts 1:9-11); immortality only through Christ (2 Tim. 1:10): the unconscious state of the dead (Eccl. 9:5, 6): the destruction of the wicked (Mal. 4:1-3); and the other kindred truths that comprise the special message of Revelation 14:6-12?

7. Is it your purpose to keep the seventh day of the week from Friday sunset to Saturday sunset as the Lord's holy day according to the fourth commandment? Luke 23:56, Ex. 20:8-11.

8. Will you practice the Bible plan for the support of God's work by rendering unto Him first the tithe, or one tenth of all your increase (Lev. 27:30: Mal 3:8-10): and then offerings as you may be able, according to His prospering hand? Deut. 16:17; Luke 6:38.

9. Is it your purpose to obey the command to eat and drink to the glory of God (1 Cor. 10:31) by abstaining from all intoxicating liquors (Prov. 23:29-32), tobacco in all its forms (1 Cor. 3:16, 17), swine's flesh (Isa. 66:15, 17), narcotics, tea, coffee, and other harmful things?

10. Are you willing to follow the Bible rule of modesty and simplicity of dress, refraining from the wearing of earrings, necklaces, bracelets, beads, rings, etc. and from any lack of dress that is out of keeping with the Bible rule of modesty? 1 Tim. 2:9, 10; 1 Peter 3:3,4; Ex. 33:5, 6; Gen 35:2-4

11. Do you believe in and have you accepted the ordinance of humility (John 13:1-17), and the ordinance of the Lord's Supper? 1 Cor. 11:23-33.

12. Is it your purpose to come out from the world and be separate in obedience to God's command in 2 Corinthians 6:17, by refraining from following the sinful practices of the world, such as dancing, card playing, theatergoing, novel reading, etc. and by shunning all questionable worldly amusements? 1 John 2:15; James 1:27; 4:4.

13. Will you seek to build up the interest of the church by giving the Sabbath School your hearty and practical support and by attending, as far as possible, all the services of the church? And will you endeavor by God's help to do your part in the work in the church? Luke 4:16; Rom. 12:4-8.

14. Do you recognize that the remnant church has the Spirit of Prophecy, and that this has been manifested to this church through the writings of Ellen G. White? Rev. 12:17; 19:10

15. Do you believe in baptism by immersion only, and are you ready to follow your Lord and Master in this sacred rite? Matt. 28:18-20; Col. 2:12; Rom. 6:3-5.

MY PURPOSE
Having given myself fully to God, and desiring to truly serve Him here and to live with Him forever, I hereby declare my acceptance of these principles of truth, and my obedience to them by His grace.

Appendix E
Baptismal Vows Commitment
1990 Church Manual

1. Do you believe there is one God: Father, Son, and Holy Spirit, a unity of three coeternal Persons?

2. Do you accept the death of Jesus Christ on Calvary as the atoning sacrifice for your sins and believe that by God's grace through faith in His shed blood you are saved from sin and its penalty?

3. Do you accept Jesus Christ as your Lord and personal Saviour believing that God, in Christ, has forgiven your sins and given you a new heart, and do you renounce the sinful ways of the world?

4. Do you accept by faith the righteousness of Christ, your Intercessor in the heavenly sanctuary, and accept His promise of transforming grace and power to live a loving, Christ-centered life in your home and before the world?

5. Do you believe that the Bible is God's inspired Word, the only rule of faith and practice for the Christian? Do you covenant to spend time regularly in prayer and Bible study?

6. Do you accept the Ten Commandments as a transcript of the character of God and a revelation of His will? Is it your purpose by the power of the indwelling Christ to keep this law, including the fourth commandment, which requires the observance of the seventh day of the week as the Sabbath of the Lord and the memorial of Creation?

7. Do you look forward to the soon coming of Jesus and the blessed hope when "this mortal shall . . . put on immortality"? As you prepare to meet the Lord, will you witness to His loving salvation, and by life and word help others to be ready for His glorious appearing?

8. Do you accept the biblical teaching of spiritual gifts and believe that the gift of prophecy is one of the identifying marks of the remnant church?

9. Do you believe in church organization? Is it your purpose to support the church by your tithes and offerings and by your personal effort and influence?

10. Do you believe that your body is the temple of the Holy Spirit; and will you honor God by caring for it, avoiding the use of that which is harmful; abstaining from all unclean foods; from the use, manufacture, or sale of alcoholic beverages; the use, manufacture, or sale of tobacco in any of its forms for human consumption; and from the misuse of or trafficking in narcotics or other drugs?

11. Do you know and understand the fundamental Bible principles as taught by the Seventh-day Adventist Church? Do you purpose, by the grace of God, to fulfill His will by ordering your life in harmony with these principles?

12. Do you accept the New Testament teaching of baptism by immersion and desire to be so baptized as a public expression of faith in Christ and His forgiveness of your sins?

13. Do you accept and believe that the Seventh-day Adventist Church is the remnant church of Bible prophecy and that people of every nation, race, and language are invited and accepted into its fellowship? Do you desire to be a member of this local congregation of the world church?